CONTENTS

Intuition for a World in Crisis
Prabhath P & Matthew C. Bronson, Editors

1   Intuiting a World in Balance
Prabhath P & Matthew C. Bronson

3   When Hearts are Joined: My Story of Exploring
Our Interconnectedness through Intuition
Henry Reed

13   The Inner Voice (Poem)
Amy I. Ramdass

14   Lost and Found: Recovering Intuition for a World in Crisis
Matthew C. Bronson & Leslie Gray

24   The Third Ventricle: Temple of the Soul
Joyce A. Kovelman & Hoang Van Duc

28   Texts by Children: Your Soul's Eye by *Alex Trux*
Facilitated by J. Ruth Gendler

29   Integral Intuitive Communion With Gaia
Prabhath P

37   Clairparlance: Activating Intuitive Communication
Matthew C. Bronson

42   Texts by Children: People Said the World Will Change in Time
Riley Felt, facilitated by J. Ruth Gendler

44   The Ecology of Intuition: From Crisis to Opportunity
Arupa L. Tesolin

49   Painting in the Sky (Poem)
Alex N. Moyer

50   Book Review: Rothberg, Donald. (2006). *The Engaged Spiritual Life:
A Buddhist Approach to Transforming Ourselves and the World.*
Jonathan S. Watts

Cover Art *Circle of Life* by Alex N. Moyer

Spring 2010 • Volume 31 • Number 2

What is ReVision?

For almost thirty years ReVision has explored the transformative and consciousness-changing dimensions of leading-edge thinking. Since its inception ReVision has been a vital forum, especially in the North American context, for the articulation of contemporary spirituality, transpersonal studies, and related new models in such fields as education, medicine, organization, social transformation, work, psychology, ecology, and gender. With a commitment to the future of humanity and the Earth, ReVision emphasizes the transformative dimensions of current and traditional thought and practice. ReVision advances inquiry and reflection especially focused on the fields presently identified as philosophy, religion, psychology, social theory, science, anthropology, education, frontier science, organizational transformation, and the arts. We seek to explore ancient ways of knowing as well as new models of transdisciplinary, interdisciplinary, multicultural, dialogical, and socially engaged inquiry. It is our intention to bring such work to bear on what appear to be the fundamental issues of our times through a variety of written and artistic modalities. In the interests of renewal and fresh vision, we strive to engage in conversation a diversity of perspectives and discourses which have often been kept separate, including those identified with terms such as Western and Eastern; indigenous and nonindigenous; Northern and Southern; feminine and masculine; intellectual; practical, and spiritual; local and global; young and old.

Artwork: Mariana Castro de Ali

Volume 31, No. 2 (ISBN 9780981970646)

ReVision (ISSN 0275-6935) is published as part of the *Society for the Study of Shamanism, Healing, and Transformation*.

Manuscript Submissions

We welcome manuscript submissions. Manuscript guidelines can be found on our webpage http://revisionpublishing.org.

POSTMASTER: Send address changes to
ReVision Publishing, P.O. Box 1855, Sebastopol, CA 95473.

Subscriptions

For subscriptions mail a check to above address or go to
www.revisionpublishing.org.

Individual Subscriptions

Subscription for one year: $36 online only,
$36 print only (international $72),
$48 print and on-line (international $84).

Subscription for two years: $60 online only,
$60 print only (international $96),
$79 print and online (international $115).

Subscription for three years: $72 online only,
$72 print only (international $108),
$96 print and online (international $132).

Institutional Subscriptions

$98 online only (international $134),
$134 print and online (international $191).

Please allow six weeks for delivery of first issue.

ReVision Abstracts

Vol. 31 No. 2   *Spring 2010*

Bronson, M. C. (2010). Clairparlance: Activating intuitive communication. *ReVision*, *31*(2), 37-41. doi:10.4298/REVN.31.2.37-41

Language is a privileged vehicle for the exploration of consciousness issues, for with our words, in large measure, we create the world we live in. With the rituals and scripts of everyday conversation, we enact the trance of reality as we know it, and inadvertently obscure a deeper well of meaning from which humanity has drawn sustenance through the ages. In this article, two linguists explore the idea of "clairparlance," intuitively inspired communication that transcends the usual subject/object dichotomy and rules of reference. They highlight examples of this "clear speaking" by sages, spiritual masters and agents of social change, with an ear to the key elements of their capacity to shift consciousness toward a wider field of human possibilities. Applications for personal development are outlined, strategies for reconnecting with the living logos that animates the world and the word.

Bronson, M. C., & Gray, L. (2010). Lost and found: Recovering intuition for a world in crisis. *ReVision*, *31*(2), 14-22. doi:10.4298/REVN.31.2.14-22

In the face of widespread alienation, despair and crisis on every front of society and the planet, how can any individual help to initiate the shifts in consciousness necessary for the continuation of life as we know and cherish it? What is the role of intuition – epitomized in the time-tested techniques of shamanism – in effecting this shift? In this dialogically constructed article a contemporary shaman and a cognitive linguist outline what has been "lost" in the transition to modernity. They explore the obstacles to coming out as an intuitive in a world dominated by the cult of rationalism and the systematic denigration of indigenous and other ways of knowing. Practical exercises and strategies for restoring balance and recovering a robust reasoning that is not divorced from intuitive states of consciousness are discussed.

Kovelman, J. A., & Duc, H. V. (2010). The third ventricle: Temple of the soul. *ReVision*, *31*(2), 24-28. doi:10.4298/REVN.31.2.24-28

The brain's ventricular system nourishes and protects the central nervous system.   Mystics believe the "True Heart" of each individual can only be approached through the Third Ventricle that serves as a gateway to hidden, invisible realms beyond our physical world. Eastern and Western scientists report that the Third Ventricle is strategically located in the exact center of the brain, beneath the Crown chakra and behind the Third Eye. As Cerebrospinal Fluid flows over the brain, a field effect is created that influences how the nervous system speaks to itself, thereby raising the possibility that the Third Ventricle and "True Heart" of the mystics mediate an as yet unrecognized role in intuition, healing, meditation, and other non-ordinary phenomena.

P, P. (2010). Integral intuitive communion with Gaia. *ReVision*, *31*(2), 29-36. doi:10.4298/REVN.31.2.29-36

Integral intuition involves accessing several interconnected dimensions existing as an integral whole. Earth is a living organism, Gaia, having physical, psychic and spiritual aspects. Humanity in its dominant practices and beliefs has lost the conscious intuitive connection and communion with the interdependent Gaian web of life, in which we are immersed. Global warming is also the result of this crisis of consciousness. This paper, explains the nature of integral intuition and Gaia, then explores how integral intuition can be applied for restoring this communion to ultimately resolve the ecological crisis. Examples of the emerging Earth-friendly worldview are presented along with the glimpse of an integral, intuitive and meditative communion with Gaia from Integral Gaia Yoga, which the author is developing.

P, P., & Bronson, M. C. (2010). Intuiting a world in balance. *ReVision*, *31*(2), 1-2. doi:10.4298/REVN.31.2.1-2

The mainstream scientific and religious discourse has discouraged intuitive capacities. There is an urgent need to broaden conventional scientific and religious approaches to integrate intuition and apply intuitive power to resolve the various challenges we face and do our part to ensure the survival and further evolution of humanity and Earth. Our authors remind us that we only need to wake up from our semi-conscious existence and access and use our intuitive treasure consciously.

Reed, H. (2010). When hearts are joined: My story of exploring our interconnectedness through intuition. *ReVision*, *31*(2), 3-13. doi:10.4298/REVN.31.2.xxx56-62

The author explores the intuitive information acquisition process through his experiments with dreams and unconscious communication between people. His personal research recalls the archetypal shamanic healing crisis followed by receiving gifts to share with others. Dream experiments discussed include replicating dream temple healings attributed to the Greek god, Asclepius, people obtaining guidance from dreams, and group dreaming, where strangers dream assistance for a stranger in distress. Subsequent experiments explored unconscious communication. Using the sound of a person's voice, listeners have daydreams that reveal information about the person speaking. Imagining making mental contact or a heart connection with another person initiated the receipt of intuitive information. The role of altruism in intuitive empathy and the value of motivated research participants are discussed.

Tesolin, A. L. (2010). The ecology of intuition: From crisis to opportunity. *ReVision*, *31*(2), 44-49. doi:10.4298/REVN.31.2.44-49

Arupa Tesolin explores how intuition positively contributes to a modern ecology of society, learning, business and the environment. The implications of introducing measured changes that foster a growing understanding of intuition's support role and causal linkages can trigger a re-orientation of global values. By collectively advancing intuition, we can create a more enlightened future for this generation and the next. Wise commitments of time, energy, research and funding in understanding the value of intuition can yield results that far outweigh the investment. Broad communication about the impact of intuition in the context of today's changes and challenges can create a progressive influence on human evolution and capability as well as improve the design of economies, societies and meaningful global cooperation.

Watts, J. S. (2010). Book Review: Donald Rothberg, *The Engaged Spiritual Life*. *ReVision*, *31*(2), 50-51. doi:10.4298/REVN.31.2.50-51

Reviews Donald Rothberg's (2006) The Engaged Spiritual Life: A Buddhist Approach to Transforming Ourselves and the World. Boston, Beacon Press. ISBN: 978-0807077252. Considers it an extremely valuable "workbook," accessible for more secularly minded social activists to help ground their activism through developing a stronger inner life and an essential volume for anyone seeking to work through relational conflicts in their daily space and to unite their personal and social concerns.

Intuiting a World in Balance
Introduction

Prabhath P & Mathew C. Bronson

Intuition is an invaluable treasure that exists deep within each individual. The dominance of a mechanistic scientific paradigm and the resultant stranglehold of analytical reasoning and the materialistic attitude towards life have caused the treasure of intuition to remain buried beneath the conscious minds of most people. Intuitive abilities are difficult to straitjacket into the rigid and static parameters of conventional scientific dogma that focuses on a rigid and reductionist subject/object division. Due to their unique nature, generally, intuitive capacities have been discouraged as

Matthew C. Bronson, Ph. D., an educational linguist and member of the executive board of ReVision, is Associate Professor in the Department of Social and Cultural Anthropology and Director of Academic Assessment at the California Institute of Integral Studies (http://www.ciis.edu) in San Francisco and a teacher educator at the University of California, Davis. His co-edited book, "So What? Now What?:The Anthropology of Consciousness Responds to a World in Crisis" will be released in Fall of 2009. He holds a B.A. and M.A, in linguistics from the University of California, Berkeley and a Ph.D. in Education from U.C. Davis. **Prabhath P** is a writer, editor, integral intuitive consultant and holistic healer based in India, who aims for the realization of an integral intuitive vision through classes, workshops, writing, art, healing and intuitive consultancy. The purpose of his life is an integral evolution of consciousness for individual and collective spiritual Enlightenment. He is now developing Integral Gaia Yoga to manifest an integral planetary Gaia consciousness. His Web site is www.envisionearth.net

unreliable by the mainstream rationalist, scientific, social, economic and political discourse of human civilization. But the religious establishment is no sanctuary: organized religion also does not encourage intuition. The religious fundamentalists want the believers to blindly obey their interpretations of the scriptures. If people listen to their inner intuitive guidance to create their destiny and commune with the Divine directly through intuition, it will erode the authority of the religious elite. In short, any widespread exercise of intuition is generally seen as a problem by both the scientific and religious authorities.

However, the dominant scientific and religious paradigms are failing increasingly before the spiraling problems that humanity is facing. In fact, the inadequacies of both rationalist and religious fundamentalism that deny and suppress the expression of inherent human potentialities like intuition, have contributed to the creation and worsening of disturbances that endanger humanity and the planet. Thus, challenges such as terrorism, sectarianism, religious fanaticism, crass commercialism, materialist fundamentalism, emergence of deadly diseases, the ecological disturbances of global warming and mass extinction are all at root, problems of limited consciousness, of limited imagination and empathy. There is an urgent need

There is an urgent need to uncover the hidden treasure of intuition by broadening the conventional scientific and religious approaches to include and integrate our intuitive capacities.

to uncover the hidden treasure of intuition by broadening the conventional scientific and religious approaches to include and integrate our intuitive capacities. The time has come to apply intuitive power to resolve the various challenges we face and do our part to ensure the survival and further evolution of humanity and Earth. Our authors remind us that we only need to wake up from our semi-conscious existence and access and use our intuitive treasure consciously:

What's Inside

Henry Reed, a prominent intuition educator opens with an account of how the dreams we experience every night can be a gateway to the deep wisdom of the unconscious mind. He shares other strategies for reconnecting with the innate intuitive capacities that we all hold and the practical wisdom of his years of experience working with individuals and groups. Psychologist Leslie Gray and linguist Matthew C. Bronson present a historical context for the suppression of intuitive modes of problem solving and explore means for recovering them through shamanistic practice and discernment in sensory experience. This recovery begins and ends in nature, so get out your walking shoes and go find some rocks that have a message for you. You'll need them for the balancing exercise described in this article.

How is the ancient capacity of intuition realized in the nervous system? Psychologist and anatomist Joyce Kovelman and medical doctor Rev. Hoang Van Duc explore the physiology of transcendence and the "Third Ventricle" in the brain, raising the possibility that it "mediate(s) an as yet unrecognized role in intuition, healing, meditation, and other non-ordinary phenomena."

Intuition and innovation trainer Arupa Tesolin shows how a revaluing of intuition is occurring in business and industry and the implications of this shift or a world in crisis. Who knew that even accountants were recognizing the value of this ancient human capacity? Hopefully, this will aid them in anticipating the next financial crisis and help us to avoid it.

Linguist Matthew C. Bronson returns with the next entry, a report on "clair-parlance," the capacity for transformative, intuitive communication manifest throughout history in spiritual masters and other charismatic speakers that is also available to us in our everyday experience. If, as Bronson claims, "language is a privileged vehicle of our relation with reality," those interested in

> **People interested in cultivating intuition and its healing powers would do well to include the study of transformative texts and speeches in their efforts.**

cultivating intuition and its healing powers would do well to include the study of transformative texts and speeches in their efforts.

His co-editor, Prabhath P points out that humanity in its dominant practices and beliefs has lost the conscious intuitive connection and communion with the interdependent Gaian web of life, in which we are immersed. He explains the nature of integral intuition and Gaia, then explores how integral intuition can be applied for restoring this communion to ultimately resolve the ecological crisis. Examples of the emerging worldview that values the web of life are presented along with the glimpse of a meditative communion with Gaia from Integral Gaia Yoga, which he is developing.

The artists have their place at the table of intuition along with scholars and practitioners. Poets Amy I. Ramdass and Alex N. Moyer round out our offering and remind us that intuition can and must be approached with the support of the Muses and not merely by the light of scholarly reason. Original paintings have been included, paintings inspired by the kinds of intuitive experiences being described. We will not be able to effectively engage the ecological, social and humanitarian crises of our times without all of our human faculties intact, including all the Muses.

When Hearts are Joined

My Story of Exploring Our Interconnectedness through Intuition

Henry Reed

This is the essential mystery of intuition: How can we learn about the external world by looking within ourselves? There must be some connection between our consciousness and the manifested universe.

Dreams, for example, have a long history of providing intuitive insights for scientific discoveries, intellectual achievements, and social movements, to name a few (Van de Castle, 1994; Moss, 2009). Dreams will be our starting point in this story of my investigations into the operation of intuition. I'll begin by describing a social dreamwork experiment. As an educational tool, this experiment has shown its value since it guarantees that most every participant will not only remember a dream, but also discover intended, desired, valid, and valuable intuitive information about a matter that was not previously conscious.

Henry Reed, Ph.D., is Professor of Transformative Studies and Practices at Atlantic University and Director of the Edgar Cayce Institute for Intuitive Studies. Author of several books and scholarly articles, he lives with his wife on a goat ranch in the Blue Ridge mountains of Virginia. His hobbies include horseback riding, driving his horse cart, and painting watercolors. To inspire intuition in others, Henry creates a mandala to share daily (www.dailymandala.blogspot.com), which is emailed to thousands of recipients. His Web site is www.henryreed.com

The Dream Helper Ceremony

To conduct this experiment, assemble seven to ten people who want to learn something about dreams. Ask for at least two people to volunteer to be a focus person, someone who voluntarily steps forward because of a pressing personal

The Visible Dream Helper Ceremony by day — Image: Henry Reed

issue, something for which they would like the group's consultative assistance. The issue is to remain undisclosed for now. The volunteers put their names into a hat for a drawing. The "luck of the draw" is dedicated to that volunteer who could best be helped by this group of dreamers. The person whose name

is drawn becomes the focus person and receives a verbal promise from each group member, "I promise, [name of focus person] to remember a dream for you tonight." Before everyone departs for bed, instructions are provided on how to recall dreams. The focus person receives instructions to write out, before going to bed, a brief statement about the issue and the help hoped for, and to bring that back when returning to hear the group's dreams. It will be read aloud to the group once they have finished processing their dreams for the focus person.

When the group reassembles, the members report their dreams. During the telling and discussion of the dreams, the focus person, who does not speak nor provide feedback to the group (sometimes turning their chair around to face away from the group) takes notes on the group's dreams and discussion. The dreamers search for patterns in the dreams, looking for commonalities in the dream that may reflect the hidden issue. As an example, consider one dream in which someone who, during a TV commercial, is about to pour cream in his coffee when he notices in the nick of time that the cream has soured, so a new carton is opened. In another dream, someone about to resume traveling as the traffic light turns green notices that a car to the right is running the red light and waits for this obstacle to clear. Here we can see the commonalities of normal, anticipated interruptions or pauses (traffic lights, TV commercials) and of unexpected, undesirable consequences of making habitual responses (drinking spoiled cream; getting hit by car), and being watchful to be able to make quick adjustments.

On the basis of the common patterns, the group begins a "profiling" analysis: What kind of life situation would stimulate dream patterns such as those observed? Is it, for example, a medical issue, a relationship conflict, or financial matter? What do the dream patterns suggest about why the person has not been able to resolve this issue? And finally, what counsel or advice seems indicated?

After the group has finished with their "diagnosis" and "prescription," the focus person then reads aloud the statement of concern that was written the night before and proceeds to give some feedback to each dreamer. Now that the group is aware of the focus person's concern, the dreams can be examined for what they might say about that focus.

The process concludes by the dreamers "taking back their dreams," to see what the dreams reflect about themselves. The usual method is for each dreamer to compose a title for their dream, to meditate on what the title reflects about them personally, and then to share in the group their answer to this question, "What am I learning about myself from my dream that may be helpful to the focus person's issue?" At the end of this sharing, it is usually clear that the focus person,

by humbly asking for help, has turned into the group's leader, initiating the dreamers into an adventure that showed them, not only their dream skills, but also an element of shared human nature. Research on the Dream Helper Ceremony or DHC (Dossey, 1992; Reed & Van de Castle, 1990; Van de Castle, 1994) has demonstrated its value along many dimensions.

Thurston (1978) conducted a cross country experiment with the DHC. More than a hundred people volunteered to dream for one of two unidentified people. They kept dream journals for one week, then for one week attempted to dream for the person whose name was sealed within an envelope. Thurston presented each focus person with the entire collection of dreams with instructions to sort them into three piles: dreams that

spoke to the issue, dreams that spoke to something in the focus person's life, and dreams that appeared to have no connection. One focus person was able to correctly sort the dreams intended for her to a statistically significant degree, and the suggestions culled from these dreams resolved her issue.

In another study, Randall (1978) showed that in an ongoing group, the DHC significantly increased dream recall. In yet another study, Walsh (1996) investigated the perceptions of group members and found that both the dreamers and the focus person perceived that the dreams were meaningful and helpful.

Most recently, researchers (Smith, DeCicco, & Moran, 2009) conducted a double-blind study in which they asked volunteers individually to dream about an undisclosed issue involving a person shown in a photo. Judges independently examined the dreams for evidence of information concerning that focus person. The results indicated that there were significantly more correlations between the dream content and the focus person's

issue than in the control dreams of these volunteers. Unfortunately, as I have found to be the case, these researchers reported that the individual dreamers could not recognize the implications of their dreams. In my group method, laypeople can effectively use the correlation among the group's dreams (the common patterns) to correctly identify the focus person's issue and its remedy on their own. Many informal lay gatherings of folks interested in dreaming have replicated these basic results innumerable times (e.g., Barasch, 2000; Brockman, 2001; Campbell, 1978; Emery, 2000; Krippner, Bogzaran, & de Carvalho, 2002; Ramos, 2009; Rishel, 1998; Van de Castle, 2004; Watts, 2002; Webb, 2000). The DHC is thus uniquely suitable for self-help groups without the assistance of dream professionals.

The DHC raises many questions for research, such as its effectiveness as a change agent, as a team building device, or as a way of introducing dream inspirations into a group or community (e.g., Brockman, 2001). My own research has pursued how one person can dream for another, and its implications for our interconnectedness.

Origins of the Dream Helper Ceremony

The DHC has an interesting history that adds to its credibility beyond the simple matter of its effectiveness as a group effect. It is both a personal story and a history of my professional research activities into the matter of intuitive communication between people. A reader might recognize elements of my story that conform to the archetype of shamanic initiation, including a healing crisis and a series of transformational experiences that also led to having gifts to share with others through applied research (McGuire, 1989 pp. 22-23; Robertson, 2000, pp. 15-20).

I was a psychology graduate student at UCLA in the late 1960's (Carlos Castaneda was an anthropology graduate student there at that time), when I ran

In the historical accounts of these temple healings, the patient would sleep in the temple and awaken in the morning recalling having had a "visitation" in the temple.

across a classmate from my undergraduate years at Pomona College, James Turrell, our senior class president. He told me some of his dreams. In one, his deceased father showed him where he could get an art studio rent free. Another dream alerted him to a distant friend who was in trouble. He had many dreams of light, which was inspiring his artistic explorations (Turrell, 2007) and later led to his receiving a MacArthur Foundation "genius award." I asked James where he learned to have these wonderful dreams. I asked, because in my graduate education at that time, dreams were viewed as a "medical sample," something you take to a doctor in private to have yourself diagnosed. James was using his dreams for personal and professional guidance. He mentioned Edgar Cayce, the "sleeping prophet" (Stearn, 1989), who claimed that everyone could learn to "dream true" (Thurston, 1989). In response to this brief remark, I intuitively envisioned a compass, and felt immediately drawn to connecting with my dreams as a way to guide me in my confused life. James offered to help me create a dream journal and begin to remember my dreams. It took me several months before I finally did remember a dream, but it changed my life (Reed, 1984). The dream suggested that my "drinking problem" was a gift to me, to help me grow. I soon was on a path of spiritual recovery from alcoholism. The dream also presaged, without my knowing it at the time, the unique method I would help others to connect with dreams.

After graduating from UCLA, I became an Assistant Professor of Psychology at Princeton University. Based upon my own experiences attempting to develop my memory for dreams (Reed, 1976a), I taught an experimental class on learning to remember dreams (Reed, 1973). I also began a program of research to see if students could direct their dreams toward particular content.

At that time, research psychologists routinely used deception as a normal part of their methodology, and the Princeton students were thus a suspicious subject population. I found the laboratory setting not conducive to the type of inspirational dreaming I'd experienced and wished to nurture in others. During a sabbatical leave, I consulted at the C.G. Jung Sleep and Dream Laboratory, in Zurich, Switzerland. The lab's director, Carl A. Meier, M.D., had recently published a book about the legends of the "dream cures" that took place in the Greek temples of Asclepius, such as at Epidaurus (Meier, 1967; Tick, 2001). In

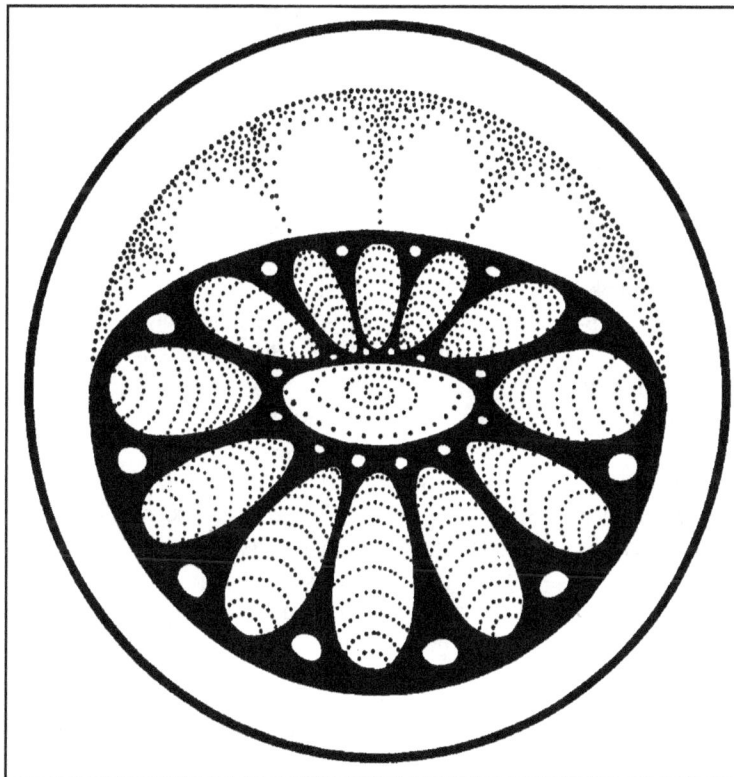

The Invisible Dream Helper Ceremony by night — Image: Henry Reed

the historical accounts of these temple healings (Edelstein & Edelstein, 1945), the patient would sleep in the temple and awaken in the morning recalling having had a "visitation" in the temple. Such visionary dreams typically involved a visit by either Asclepius himself, or one of his animal helpers (a dog or snake). During the nocturnal visitation, some kind of "treatment" would occur, and the person would awaken cured. Some of the testimonies of these treatments seem bizarre or symbolic, such as being bitten by Asclepius' snake. Meier noted that Hippocrates, the father of modern

medicine, claimed that all his remedies originated in the recorded healings of Asclepius, which is perhaps why today the symbol for medicine is Asclepius' staff and snake. I wanted to replicate the phenomenon of these visionary temple dreams. Meier, however, was conducting experiments of a more mechanistic bent, such as having a person sleep in a cold room to see if the person would have dreams involving more physical activity, as a means of compensating for the cold environment. I fulfilled my consultation obligations by designing for the lab a set of alternative, more humanistic methods of exploring dreams, and then returned to Princeton to follow my own course of research into temple-incubated dreams.

I had become acquainted with Edgar Cayce's organization in Virginia Beach, the Association for Research and Enlightenment, and I received an invitation to conduct dream research with young people at A.R.E.'s summer camp in the Blue Ridge mountains. Taking a cue from my own initiatory dream, I used a tent as my outdoor dream temple and began my attempt to revive the ancient phenomenon of dream incubation. I employed a combination of isolation, meditation, psychodrama (involving the two archetypal themes of the sacred place and visitation of the divine benefactor), and pre-sleep suggestion in an attempt to recreate in the mind of the incubant something similar to what might have occurred to an ancient one preparing to sleep in one of Asclepius' temples (Reed, 1976b). Many folks did have inspiring dreams that subsequently shaped their future. One young lad drowning in drug problems had a classic heroic dream of carving his own path through the forest with a sword. Some even had the type of visionary visitation dream recorded from ancient testimonies. For example, one lady dreamed that she awakened in the middle of the night to find herself sleeping in the open, as a strong wind had blown the tent away! A little woman hopped out of the bushes, took her by the hand, and flew her way up into the sky where the lady showed the dreamer

Daydreaming to a voice — Image: Henry Reed

several stone tablets outlining her past, present and future lives. She then awoke again to find herself tucked in her sleeping bag safely inside the tent.

Julian Jaynes (who was a drinking buddy of mine at Princeton) called visitation dreams such as this one "bicameral," (Jaynes, 1976). His research suggested that in Biblical times and before, brain function was different than it is today. He attributed ancient accounts of hearing voices and visionary dreams (meaning that these dreams seem to occur right where the person was sleeping) to the effect of one cerebral hemisphere communicating with the other. He speculated that as the brain developed, the left hemisphere became dominant, and the right became silent, ushering in a more rational consciousness as we know it today. My research, however, showed that such bicameral dreams were still possible today, given the correct circumstances. Given that such dreams represent a different form of brain functioning, it is not unreasonable to assume that biophysical effects related to healing, such as changes in DNA, might occur in such dreams (Rossi, 2000, 2004). Two researchers followed up on my work by using dream incubation to treat sinusitis (Kwako, 1978) and poor eyesight (West, 1979).

When I submitted my report on the dream tent to the *Journal of Humanistic Psychology*, the editor, Tom Greening, Ph.D., accepted it without revision (Reed, 1976b). A psychiatrist writing about the religious potential in dreams (Gunter, 1983) wrote of my work that it shows "...there is in our psyche a religious energy available to our consciousness as religious images and symbols in dreams" (p. 425).The psychology faculty at Princeton had a different opinion of my work: they expelled me for demonstrating, by my introducing something akin to "prayer" in the incubation ceremony, that I had no intention of pursuing research in a "scientific" manner. Thus ended my career in traditional academia, leaving me free to follow other dreams.

Upon my first visit to the A.R.E. in Virginia Beach, for example, I had a dream where a group of people were exploring how to "conduct research into enlightenment." The dream concluded with the group dancing to create a fountain of sparks that lit their space. Each dancer displayed a personal symbol that contributed to the enlightenment (Reed, 1976b). The dream proved valuable in my research. I devised a home-study dream research project (Reed, 1978; Reed, 2005) to see if lay-people could make constructive use of their dreams by following this intriguing proposal from the Edgar Cayce material: If you will apply any insights you believe you are perceiving in your dream by taking action on them, you will have subsequent dreams that will correct your experimental action, and dream by dream, application by application, your dreams will teach you how to interpret them to reach a constructive goal (Thurston, 1989). The results of this home-study project supported this principle (Reed, 1978). Moreover, the feedback from the hundreds of participants evidenced their great enthusiasm for doing dreamwork on their own. Many participants had uplifting and instructive stories to tell (Albright, 2008; Bailey, 2007; Dwyer, 2000; Gravallese, 2000; King, 2008; Roberts, 2007; van Vliet, 2000; Wessling, 2000).

During this time, I had a dream where a letter arrived in my Princeton University faculty mailbox (although I was no longer on the faculty), addressed to me as "To Henry Reed, c/o Sundance College." I researched the meaning of Sundance, to learn that it was a Native American spiritual ceremony, involving a circle of dancers, seeking visions for the good of the community with an archetypal theme similar to the Celtic May Pole dance (Reed, 1987). From that dream, I was led to create *Sundance: The Community Dream Journal* (see Reed, 1976c), publishing stories of dreamwork successes by lay people. Years later, when the International Association for the Study of Dreams was formed, their official history mentioned the *Sundance* journals as one of the impetuses for creating the organization. When McGuire (1989, p. 22) wrote, "By common agreement, the father of the modern dreamwork movement is Henry Reed," it was because the success of the *Sundance* journals showed that there was a large lay population that were using their dreams for personal insight, growth, and life planning, thus rescuing dreams from psychotherapy while inspiring the creation of the International Association for the Study of Dreams (McGuire, 1989; Ossana, 2009). The dream of the research dance had yet further to offer.

At A.R.E. camp, I made a serendipi-

The research dance — Image: Henry Reed

tous discovery. Young people not sleeping in the "dream tent" would tell me their dreams from time to time and I noticed that several of these dreams contained veiled, symbolic references to the focus issue of the person who had slept in the dream tent the night before. In this supportive atmosphere, emphasizing cooperation and interpersonal goodwill, these young folks seemed to be vicariously participating in an incubant's dream tent experience. Partly out of curiosity, partly out of a sense of camaraderie, and partly from an unconscious sense of identification with the incubant's issues, these folks were having "bystander dreams." Here was a case of apparent spontaneous "psychic" dreaming arising from some kind of Good Samaritan spirit. But could this phenomenon be re-created intentionally?

In consultation with Robert Van de Castle, who at the time was on the medical faculty of the University of Virginia, and who had served successfully many times as a telepathic perceiver in the famous Maimonides dream ESP experiments (Ullman, Krippner, & Vaughan, 1973), I learned from Bob that he often had dreams in the ESP lab that did not concern the target picture the agent was studying all night, but concerned instead personal problems the agent was experiencing. Bob was encouraging that the A.R.E. camp youth would respond positively to a dream ESP task that would involve connecting with an undisclosed problem of a fellow camper. I used my dream of the research dance to structure the experiment. Bob and I conducted the first dream helper ceremonies at camp, to great effect (Reed & Van de Castle, 1990; Van de Castle, 1994). Together with the implications of the *Sundance* journals, the DHC provided a new avenue for groups or communities to find inspirations for their shared ventures (Brockman, 2001; Reed, 1977, 1987).

As my confidence grew in the repeatability and usefulness of the DHC process, I began to question how someone actually dreams for another person. I intuited that the process went something like this: A dreamer would make an empathic connection with the focus person. Doing so, the dreamer would then

be experiencing some of the same dilemma feelings of the focus person. These feelings, acting somewhat like an inoculant, would then stimulate the dreamer to have a dream to resolve those feelings. It was as if the dreamer were saying, "When I imagine being in your predicament, what it brings up for me is thus and so, and how I see to deal with that is by this and that."

The Intimacy of Intuitive Listening

A serendipitous event one day in my counseling practice led me to begin to create waking analogies to the DHC. One afternoon a client and I stumbled onto an important lesson. It was after lunch and I was feeling sleepy. The client began the session, as usual, with a recount of the week's injustices, etc., while I relaxed and floated along the sound of his voice. Suddenly, I felt myself jerk, and I realized I had lost consciousness momentarily (therapists never actually fall asleep on the job!). I reflected that I had been absorbed in a personal memory of locating a baby bird who had fallen out of its nest in my back yard. My attempts to feed it were thwarted by its constant,

If you will apply any insights you believe you are perceiving in your dream by taking action on them, you will have subsequent dreams that will correct your experimental action.

fearful chirping. To regain a connection with my client's disclosures, I asked him how he felt about the week's soap opera, and he replied that it hurt that folks did not listen to him, or pay him much attention, and it reminded him of when he was a young child with his mom at a department store. He had become separated from her and was wandering lost in the store. A saleswoman noticed him, and taking him into the back room to find help, she said, "here's a baby bird fallen out of his nest." When I heard him say that, I realized that somehow during my reverie, we had made

an important connection. We discussed both my feelings and his, our memories, and discussed how his own cries for help sometimes prevented his getting help.

The dream tent — Image: Henry Reed

Later I reflected that what had transpired was similar to the DHC, as I had, as the "dreamer," come up with something from my past that connected with the client. I felt that our experience was similar to that described in the literature of hypnosis experiments in the nineteenth century (Dingwall, 1967), called "rapport," in which the hypnotist's induction made the client somewhat psychic for the hypnotist's unconscious. It was through such a process at that time that "medical clairvoyants" were popular and also led to the laboratory investigations into ESP.

On the basis of a voice generated rapport, I developed a waking analogy to the DHC (Reed, 1994). In this experimental interaction, a group of seven to eight people sit close together in a circle. One person takes a turn to be the "focus" person, and voices a tone, such as "Ahhhh...." while the others in the group intone the same sound, as if they are using the focus person's sound as a basis for intuitive listening. Then the focus person begins to count aloud, backwards, from 99 to 1, while the group members close their eyes and allow the sound of the person's voice to wash over them and to induce daydreams. After the countdown, the group members share their experiences, look for commonalities, and then receive feedback from the focus person as to how these daydreams related to the focus person. We called it the "Getting to Know You Game" when the intuitive listeners were simply attempting to gain some impressions about the speaker. We called it the "Psychic Detective Game" if we asked the focus person to set a secret intention of hoping to get insight into a personal dilemma from the group's daydreams, as in DHC. Although when first learning the process, listeners found it awkward and a bit nervously amusing, by the time they had finished exploring the process with everyone having a turn at being a focus person, they were generally amazed at the meaningfulness of the results— "uncanny" being a common remark (Reed, 1994). When I submitted my report to the *Journal of the American Society for Psychical Research*, some reviewers felt that no face-to-face interactions could be called "psychic," but the journal's editor, Rhea White, Ph.D. said the study stood as a "dark star in parapsychology" (personal communication, November, 1995).

Two important insights into intuition came about in this study. First of all, we observed that the "listeners" experienced two distinct yet overlapping states of consciousness during their reveries. In one state, the listener would hear the focus person's counting, and might experience thoughts about the focus person. In the other state, the listener would be absorbed in a reverie and be less conscious of the focus person's counting. In the first state, there was a clear sense of separation between listener and speaker, while in the second state, it was as if the listener had become merged with the speaker. During the induction produced by the focus person's vocalization, listeners would vacillate between these two states, one a conscious, sensory awareness, and the other something akin to a semi-hypnotized, pre-sleep state with the imagination more active than the senses. Experiences occurring in the conscious state were more like observations or

judgments ("the focus person sounded nervous when she counted"), whereas the experiences in the subconscious state were more like subjective, often symbolic, reflections of the listener's response to the voice ("I was sliding down some stairs...").

There has been sufficient research into the fear of ESP (Tart, 1984, 1986a, 1986b) to know that one concern is about the loss of boundaries and unwanted intimacy. On the other hand, research

There is a long tradition that attributes to the heart, as a synonym for the intuitive imagination, to perceive "subtle energy" or similar phenomena that are not visible to the senses.

has shown that spontaneous ESP occurs more often among intimates than among strangers (Rhine, 1981; Stevenson, 1970). In my experiments, strangers find themselves in a situation that invites immediate intimacy. Reports from many participants revealed that the intimacy inherent in the listening process presented challenges. Some participants would privately tell me that when they began to listen to the person's voice, they got some bad feelings, and so withdrew from the process. Others reported having emotions or physical sensations that persisted afterwards. These reports gave clear examples of what has been called "emotional contagion," (Hatfield et al., 1994), where one person can "pick up" the emotions of another person and be affected by them, usually as a result of unconscious mimicry. It would seem that this experimental process set up emotional resonance between participants. The effect of the resonance, just as in my spontaneous experience in my counseling session, was that the listener would be "reminded" of personal stuff that was resonant with the speaker.

It seemed as if interpersonal intuition, of which I observed a lot in these experiments of intuitive listening, was an immediate potentiality, and that personal

feelings about intimacy played a role in allowing these connections to be experienced. I realized that the use of the voice was probably sufficient but not necessary to instigate these connections. The essential element was the implicit mimicry of the focus person by the listeners.

Experiencing the Presence of Another Mind

In my next investigation, I explored the experience of simply being in "mental contact" with another person, to see if the experience of mental contact itself is intuitively given and whether it provides a channel for intuitive communication. I called this next experimental interaction, the "Close to You" process (Reed, 1996a; Reed, 1996b). I had participants in pairs, sitting facing each other. I gave instructions for them to take turns making faces and moving their hands about while the other person pretended to be the first person's reflection in the mirror. Thus they took turns mimicking the other person's facial expressions and hand movements. Folks generally laughed and played happily at this non-verbal activity. After a couple of minutes, I would ask them to close their eyes and put their hands in their laps. I then would give this instruction: "Gradually and gently allow yourself to become aware of the feeling of the presence of your partner. Imagine that you can reach out psychically and make mental contact with your partner. As you experience making mental contact with your partner, notice what you experience. Just allow your experience to happen by itself without your trying to experience anything in particular, just observe the spontaneous stream of your consciousness" (see Reed, 1996a, or Reed, 1996c for texts of inductions used). At the end of three minutes of silence, I would ask them to open their eyes and share with their partner what they experienced.

It is such a simple exercise, but the results are quite enlightening. First of all, most every participant agreed that the experience of "mental contact" *felt real!* This phenomenological reality will prove, I believe, to be one of the most important results of this experiment. The participants also agreed that the short period of imagined mental contact felt intimate, and they responded to the experience of intimacy in ways recognizable to those familiar with intimacy issues: they often felt shy about entering into the "mental contact" experience, but once they felt comfortable, they liked it and were reluctant to let it go. They often changed their feelings about their partner, going from the judgments of first impressions, to a more heartfelt acceptance and empathy for the other person. Some formed longer term attachments to their partner, friendships, correspondence, etc., based upon this brief encounter. Past research has shown that when two people "tune into" each other, there is a correlation among their EEG responses (Grinberg-Zylberbaum, & Ramos, J., 1987; Grinberg-Zylberbaum et al., 1993) and in their heart response (McCraty, 2004). As much as these external phenomena are suggestive, the participants' own reports of their mutual, interlocking, or correlated experiences gave them experiential evidence that their shared experience was more than "just imagination." In variations of the method, where one partner would play the role of a focus person dwelling on an undisclosed problem, the other partner experienced reveries that proved helpful to the focus person (see Reed, 1996b for details of these correspondences).

During the three minute period of silent "mental contact" there was evidence from their reports of the kind of vacillation between two states of mind we observed in the intuitive listening experiments. In one state, the person would experience "energy" going between the two partners. Here we have the clear sense of separation of the two participants. In the other state, the person would experience daydreaming or reveries, with or without the inclusion of the partner in the imagery, but without the sense of spatial separation from the partner. As in the previous experiments, the participants didn't usually recognize the meaningfulness of their reverie until

they compared notes with their partner. Thus these daydreams often evidenced what therapists call an "inter-subjective" reality (Stolorow, Atwood, & Brandchaft, 1994), in which the two partners were processing the same reality but from their individual, subjective point of view. The "objective" knowledge was hidden within subjective expression. They came to know something of the other person by looking within themselves, yet the knowledge was not evident to them, because it seemed so totally subjective and "imaginary."

When the participants in our research withdrew from the "mental contact" with their partner, they felt separate again, until I would ask them, "are you and your partner still joined, or separated?" The answer would depend upon whether they looked at their partner, three feet away, or "felt" their partner, at which they realized that with their "feeling-imagination," they could still perceive the connection. It would seem that whether or not we experience ourselves

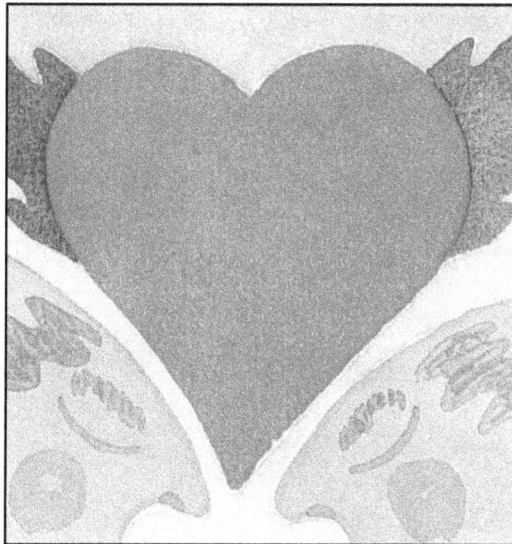

Two heads, one heart — Image: Henry Reed

as separate from one another or connected with each other depends upon which system of awareness we use: our sense perceptions or our feeling/imagination. As Albert Einstein is quoted as saying, "Our separation from each other is an optical illusion of consciousness" (Powell, 2009, p. 46). The mystery of how we become aware of the presence of other minds seems solved: we do so intuitively, from within.

My "Close to You" experiments rep-

licated much in the clinical literature that reframes "counter-transference" as an intuitive, unconscious communicative response to the client that contains objective information about the client in the form of a subjective manifestation of empathy. Researchers describe an "imaginal realm," where images from daydreams are somehow a reflection of a "subtle energy" interaction between two persons, calling the space in between the "interactive field" (Spiegelman & Mansfield, 1996; Stein, 1995). Helping me with extensive rewriting, the editor of the *Journal of Analytical Psychology*, John Beebe, M.D., called the paper I submitted a "minor classic" (personal communication, February, 1994), and a reviewer (Schwartz-Salant, 1998, p. 25) called it "seminal," because it showed that these clinical phenomena could be quickly induced between strangers. Many of my respondents reported imagery that corresponds to what researchers describe concerning these kinds of subtle energy interactions (Collinge, 1998).

The Intuitive Heart Discovery Process

Many of the participants in my research have mentioned that making a "heart connection" with their partners erased the illusion of separateness. Indeed, our language has many examples of the use of the word heart as a metaphor for intuition, as in "I know in my heart," and for intuitive connections, such as "My heart reached out to him" (Reed & English, 2000). There is a long tradition that attributes to the heart, as a synonym for the intuitive imagination, to perceive "subtle energy" or similar phenomena that are not visible to the senses (Corbin, 1972; Schwartz-Salant, 1998). In my "Close to You" experiment, I created a quick, artificial relationship by having them mimic each other in a fun, spontaneous manner, followed by a period in which all sensory contact was removed. Yet these participants experienced, under the guise of imagined mental contact that their interaction with their partner continued at some other level, and it was something that they could monitor and to which they responded. Their mental contact felt real — real enough to make a difference to them. It seems natural for folks to be able to create an intuitive, empathic connection with another person when they care to do so. To test this idea, I developed my most recent experiment, the "Intuitive Heart Discovery Process."

I first developed a brief meditative induction to create an "open heart." The induction begins with the use of an affirmation from Autogenic Therapy, "it breathes me," which shifts the person from an ego state of self-control, to a more passive, spontaneous state of trusting "inspiration" (Luthe & Schultz, 1969). The second stage asks the person to give thanks for each incoming breath, in order to induce a state of gratitude, which then creates a "heart coherence," (Childre & Martin, 1999; McArthur, & McArthur, 1997). Together, these steps deconstruct the ego to becoming a state of transparent, passive, and grateful witnessing of the spontaneous flow of experience (see Reed, 1996c, pp. 28-29 for text of induction; audio recording at Reed, 2007). The Intuitive Heart Discovery Process begins with this induction, followed by instructions to allow a memory to spontaneously come to mind. The memory will be used as a metaphor to understand the intended target. In this experiment, involving pairs of participants, each partner takes a turn at being the "seeker," who intends to receive intuitive guidance on an undisclosed issue, and at being the "intuitive consultant," who intends to look within for a seed of wisdom that can provide the guidance. The essence of this experiment, however, is that the consultant will retrieve a personal memory of a specific incident from the past, and use it as a metaphorical teaching story. Here is an example of the type of exchange that ensues:

Pepe served as the intuitive while Jorge secretly intended a focus for Pepe's assistance. After the induction, Pepe recalled a time when he was a young boy and his father, who worked and lived so far away that he came home only once a year, made a surprise visit. Pepe was without a father most of the time and got used to playing by himself.

He was playing with his toys when his father unexpectedly arrived. "My father walked over to see my toys on the floor and he was pleased with what I was making with them. We played together and it was really fun!" He reflected upon the memory and told Pepe that it was good that he could play alone and make himself feel contented. When his father came, it was very special, but he had to learn to help himself and that was very good. Jorge's question was, "Should I start up my new business with selling greeting cards?" He explained, "I asked you this question because I prayed to God about this new business but God didn't answer. Your story makes me realize something very important. Always I am praying to God about something, about this or that problem, getting angry with God that I don't get an answer when I need it. I need to learn, like you did, the value of doing for myself. Then when God appears, it will be like a gift!" Jorge reported a week later that he had started up his business and was really happy about it. "Our talk was not just words," Pepe said, "but made a difference in my

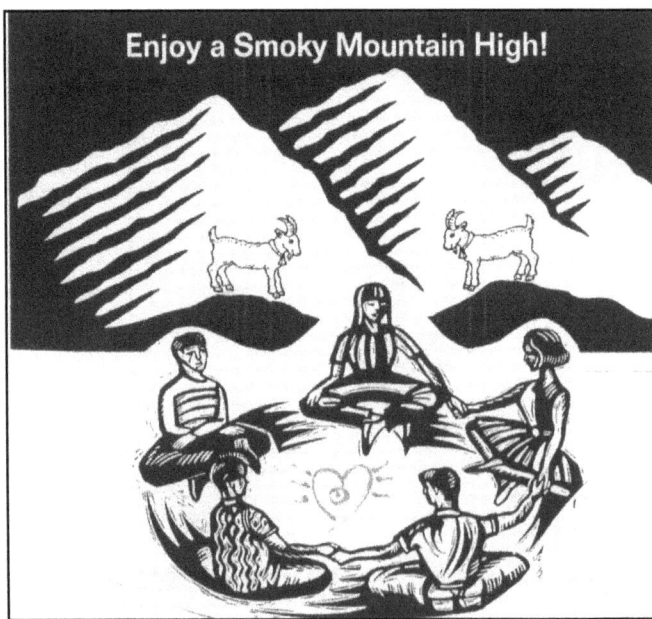

Enjoy a Smoky Mountain High!

An intuitive heart group — Image: Henry Reed

friend's life" (Reed, 1998).

Reflections

One of the recurring themes in these experiments is that a person may receive intuitive information in a subjective form, often without recognizing it as such. Stephen Harrod Buhner (2004)

noted a similar process in his experiments attempting to learn from plants about their potential medicinal value. He found that while meditating on the plant, he would have reveries that he could interpret to give him the needed information. It is a process that I have replicated (Reed, 2008). As this intuitive, subjective form of information gathering and processing has gained more attention in recent years it has acquired the term, "enchantment," (Moore, 1996). The term has pertinent connotations, as the intuitive induction is subliminal (the person is unaware that it is transpiring) and it stimulates and shapes the perceiver's own daydreaming and memory processes, so that the person unwittingly becomes under the "spell" of the source. What is significant to our investigations is that during such communication, there is no sense of separation between perceiver and perceived, unlike "objective" intuition which involves a separation between subject and object ("*I* know *this* about *you*!").

A second theme is that all my experiments involve two or more people being intuitive together. If it is true that we are all naturally intuitive, that capacity needs less training than does our socialization regarding sharing intuitions. In my experiments, the perceiver(s) have been unaware of the specifics of the target focus, and when the intuitive "impressions" are shared, both perceiver(s) and the focus person work together to see "the patterns that connect," to use a description of intuition provided by Gregory Bateson (2002). These experiments have led to a manual for a self-help group wishing to study intuition (Reed, 1996c). Scores of groups have independently used this manual to successfully replicate the basic findings I've described here. A consistent topic of feedback from these folks is that they formerly considered intuitions as a private matter with "no credentials," but have learned that in a supportive social environment, where altruism motivates the exercises, they can share and validate their intuitions while they provide inspiration and guidance to one another. Edgar Cayce suggested there was great value in the small group for exploring intuition (Cayce, 1996; Schwartz, 2008) and these experiments provide such a context in which his favored method, the correlating of impressions, provides a method for social consensus regarding intuitive information.

Most parapsychological experiments ask participants to attempt a task merely to see if they can succeed at it, their being no other motivation involved. The procedures also typically avoid or eliminate any interpersonal link between the focus person and the perceiver. Edgar Cayce stressed the importance of maintaining the emotional link between the participants and developing the motivation to communicate across the unconscious psychic connection (Reed, 1996d). In the experiments reported here, perceivers may have had some ego concerns about recalling any dreams or experiencing any impressions, but their core focus was on making an effort to be helpful. Altruism is practical spirituality and is a wonderful way to help people stretch beyond ego to express the abilities of a greater self. Finally, in contrast to most cases of employing paid research subjects, the participants in my experiments were all paying participants in workshops devoted to helping people explore their intuition—the participants funded the research. It was Sydney Jourard (1971) who inspired me to adopt this collaborative approach, emphasizing dialogue between researcher and participant co-researchers.

Finally, what have I learned about how we can understand the external world by turning within? (Goldberg, 1983) surveyed intuitive practices to find that a common strategy is to "become one with" the target of one's intuition. Experiencing intuitions about a target through grateful heart awareness suggests that when hopes, fears and thinking are abandoned, being in harmony with the truth and beauty of "what is," including the target, fulfills the intent. Musical metaphors are common for this effect, such as "resonance," (Metzner, 1987). Engineering provides the metaphor of "entrainment" (McCraty, 2004). Chaos theory provides the metaphor of "strange

attractor" (Robertson, 2009). I prefer to think in terms of the phenomenology of human experience, namely *meaning* (de Quincey, 2009). Somehow our participants were able to achieve moments of shared meaning. Jung's concept of synchronicity (Jung, 1973; Mansfield, 1995, 2002) may apply to such meaningful correspondences, but the correlations in our experiments were *intentional* and employed no external tools. Yet divination is the closest existing model concerning intended synchronicities. Divination assumes that the diviner becomes one with "divine order," and through this alignment, provides intuitive guidance consistent with it; thus divination is also based upon a harmony/resonance metaphor. The phrase, "when hearts are joined, no words are needed," perhaps anticipates those theorists who claim that there is but one root consciousness shared by all creation (Goswami, 1993), such that a heart-directed *intention* to intuitively empathize with any external reality seems sufficient to direct access to the desired information. What gives intentionality such seemingly magical powers? We must continue to search within ourselves for answers to such questions and share our impressions with others.

References

Albright, G. S. (2008). Better than the movies: My dream quest. *Intuitive-Connections Network*, September. Retrieved May 1, 2009, from http://intuitive-connections.net/2008/albrightdreamquest.htm

Bailey, D. (2007). A story of a dream quest. *Intuitive-Connections Network*, March. Retrieved May 1, 2009, from http://www.intuitive-connections.net/2007/baileydreamquest.htm

Barasch, M. I. (2000). *Healing dreams: Exploring the dreams that can change your life.* New York: Riverhead Books.

Bateman, G. (2002). *Mind and nature: A necessary unity.* Cresskill, NY: Hampton Press.

Brockman, P. C. (2001). *The community dream: Awaking the Christian tribal consciousness.* Boulder, CO: Woven Word Press.

Buhner, S. H. (2004). *The secret teaching of plants: The intelligence of the heart in the direct perception of nature.* Rochester, VT: Bear & Co.

Campbell, J. (1978). *Dreams beyond dreaming.* Marceline, MO: Walsworth Publishing.

Cayce, E. (1996). *A search for God: Books 1&2.* Virginia Beach, VA: A.R.E. Press.

Childre, D. & Martin, H. (1999). *The heartmath solution.* San Francisco, CA: HarperSanFrancisco.

Clark, D. (2007). Leaving old ways at ease: A story of a dream quest. *Intuitive-Connections Network*, December. Retrieved May 1, 2009 from http://www.intuitive-connections.net/2007/dreamquest-clark.htm

Collinge, W. (1998). *Subtle energy: Awakening to the unseen forces in our lives.* New York: Warner Books.

Corbin, H. (1972). Mundus Imaginalis: or the Imaginary and the imaginal. *Spring: An Annual of Archetypal Psychology and Jungian Thought.* Dallas, TX: Spring Publications, 1-19.

De Quincy, C. (2008). *Consciousness from zombies to angels: The shadow and the light of knowing who you are.* Rochester, VT: Park Street Press.

Dingwall, E. (Ed.). (1967). *Abnormal hypnotic phenomena: A survey of nineteenth century cases.* London: Churchill.

Dossey, L. (1992). *Reinventing Medicine: Beyond mind-body to a new era of healing.* New York: HarperCollins.

Dwyer, M. (2000). There's no need to go outside for better seeing. In Reed, H. *Dream solutions! Dream realizations: The original dream quest guidebook trailblazing intuitive dream guidance* (pp. 30-37). Rancho Mirage, CA: WePublishBooks. Copy retrieved May 1, 2009, from http://www.intuitive-connections.net/2002/dwyer.htm

Edelstein, E.J., & Edelstein, L. (1945). *Asclepius: A collection and interpretation of the testimonies* (Vols. 1-2). Baltimore: Johns Hopkins Press.

Emery, M. (2000). *The intuitive healer: Accessing your inner physician.* New York: St. Martins.

Goldberg, P. (1983). *The intuitive edge: Understanding intuition and applying it in everyday life.* Los Angeles: Tarcher.

Goswami, A. (1993). *The self-aware universe.* Los Angeles: Tarcher.

Gravallese, J. (2000). Life force exploding: A dream quest experience. In Reed, H. *Dream solutions! Dream realizations: The original dream quest guidebook trailblazing intuitive dream guidance* (pp. 37-45). Rancho Mirage, CA: WePublishBooks. Copy retrieved May 1, 2009, from http://www.intuitive-connections.net//issue2/quest.htm

Grinberg-Zylberbaum, J., & Ramos, J. (1987). Patterns of interhemispheric correlation during human communication. *International Journal of Neuroscience, 36,* 41-53.

Grinberg-Zylberbaum, J., et al. (1993). Human communication and the electrophysiological activity of the brain. *Subtle Energies,* Vol. 3, No. 3, 25-43.

Gunter, P.R. (1983). Religious dreaming: A viewpoint. *American Journal of Psychotherapy, 37*(3), 411-427.

Hatfield, E., et al. (1994). *Emotional contagion: Studies in emotion and social interaction.* Cambridge: Cambridge University Press.

Jaynes, J. (1976). *The origin of consciousness in the breakdown of the bicameral mind.* New York: Wiley.

Jourard, S. (1971). *The transparent self.* New York: Van Nostrand.

Jung, C. G. (1973). *Synchronicity: An acausal connecting principle.* Princeton, NJ: Princeton University Press.

King, L. S. (2008). Shoe dreams on my dream quest. *Intuitive-Connections Network*, January. Retrieved May 1, 2009, from http://www.intuitive-connections.net/2008/dreamquestking.htm

Krippner, S., Bogzaran, F., & de Carvalho, A. P. (2002). *Extraordinary dreams and how to work with them*. New York: S.U.N.Y. Press.

Kwako, J. (1978). Dream therapy for sinusitis. *Sundance: The Community Dream Journal*, 2(2), 248-251.

Luthe, W., & Schultz J. H. (1969). *Autogenic Therapy*. New York: Grune & Stratton.

Mansfield, V. (1995). *Synchronicity, science and soul-making: Understanding Jungian synchronicity through physics, Buddhism, and philosophy*. Chicago: Open Court.

Mansfield, V. (2002). *Head and heart: A personal exploration of science and the sacred*. Wheaton, IL: Quest Books.

McArthur, D., & McArthur, B. (1997). *The intelligent heart: Transform your life with the laws of love*. Virginia Beach, VA: A.R.E. Press.

McCraty, R. (2004). The energetic heart: Bioelectromagnetic communication within and between people. In P. J. Rosch, & M. S. Markov, (Eds.), *Clinical applications of bioelectromagnetic medicine* (pp. 541-562). New York: Marcel Dekker.

McGuire, J. (1989). *Night and day: Use the power of your dreams to transform your life*. New York: Simon & Schuster.

Meier, C.A. (1967). *Ancient incubation and modern psychotherapy*. Evanston: Northwestern University Press.

Metzner, R. (1987). Resonance as metaphor and metaphor as resonance. *ReVision*, 10(1), 37-44.

Moore, T. (1996). *The re-enchantment of everyday life*. New York: HarperCollins.

Moss, R. (2009). *The secret history of dreaming*. Novato, CA: New World Library.

Ossana, R. (2009). *History of dream network*. Retrieved May 1, 2009, from www.understandthemeaningofmydreams.com/cgi-bin/article/news.cgi?act=read&cat=11&num=2

Powell, D. H. (2009). *The ESP enigma: The scientific case for psychic phenomena*. New York: Walker & Co.

Ramos, H. V. (2009). *Testimonials*. Retrieved May 1, 2009, from http://heleneramos.com/?page_id=14

Randall, A. (1978). Dream sharing and shared metaphors in a short term community (Doctoral dissertation, Columbia University Teachers College, 1978). *Dissertation Abstracts International*, DAI-B 39/06, p. 3002, Dec 1978.

Reed, H. (1973). Learning to remember dreams. *Journal of Humanistic Psychology*, 1973, 13, 33-48. Reprint retrieved May 1, 2009, from http://www.henryreed.com/learnrememberdreams.pdf

Reed, H. (1976a). The art of remembering dreams. *Quadrant*, 9, 48-60. Reprint retrieved May 1, 2009, from http://www.henryreed.com/artrememberdreams.pdf

Reed, H. (1976b). Dream incubation: A reconstruction of a ritual in contemporary form. *Journal of Humanistic Psychology*, 16, 53-70. Reprint retrieved May 1, 2009, from http://www.henryreed.com/incubation.pdf

Reed, H., Ed. (1976c). The A.R.E. Dream Research Project. *Sundance: The Community Dream Journal*, 1(1), 27-45. Reprint retrieved May 1, 2009, from http://www.creativespirit.net/Sundance-1-1/27.htm

Reed, H. (1977). Sundance: Inspirational dreaming in community. In J. Long, (Ed.), *Extrasensory Ecology: Parapsychology and Anthropology* (pp. 155-187). Metuchen, NJ: Scarecrow Press.

Reed, H. (1978). Improved dream recall associated with meditation. *Journal of Clinical Psychology*, 34, 150-156. Reprint retrieved May 1, 2009, from http://www.henryreed.com/meditationdreamrecall.pdf

Reed, H. (1984). From alcoholic to dreamer. *Voices*, Spring, 20(1), 62-29. Copy retrieved May 1, 2009 from http://www.henryreed.com/reed/publications/gethelpdreams.php

Reed, H. (1987). The Sundance experiment. In R. Russo, (Ed.), *Dreams are wiser than men* (pp. 334-344). Berkeley, CA: North Atlantic Books.

Reed, H. (1994). Intimacy and Psi: An initial exploration. *Journal of the American Society for Psychical Research*, 88, 327-360. Reprint retrieved May 1, 2009, from http://www.henryreed.com/getknowyou.pdf

Reed, H. (1996a). Close encounters in the liminal zone: Explorations in imaginal communication, part 1. *Journal of Analytical Psychology*, 41, 81-116. Reprint retrieved May 1, 2009, from http://www.henryreed.com/close2you1.pdf

Reed, H. (1996b). Close encounters in the liminal zone: Explorations in imaginal communication, part 2. *Journal of Analytical Psychology*, 41, 203-226. Reprint retrieved May 1, 2009, from http://www.henryreed.com/close2you2.pdf

Reed, H. (1996c). *Exercise your intuitive heart: Develop another way of knowing*. Mouth of Wilson, VA: Hermes Home Press.

Reed, H. (1996d). *Awakening your psychic powers: Open your inner mind and control your psychic intuition today (Edgar Cayce guides)*. New York: St. Martins Press.

Reed, H. (1998). Rituals of the intuitive heart. *Intuition*, January/February, 9, 54-56. Copy retrieved May 1, 2009, from http://www.intuitiveheart.com/discovery.htm

Reed, H. (2005). *Dream solutions! Dream realizations: The original dreamquest guidebook trailblazing intuitive dream guidance*. Rancho Mirage, CA: WePublishBooks. (Republished 2009 by Hermes Home Press, available at http:www.lulu.com/content/570130)

Reed, H. (2007). The inspired heart. Audio recording retrieved May 1, 2009, from http://www.heart-awareness.com/ih.mp3

Reed, H. (2008). It's the spirit that heals. *Venture Inward*, November/December, 45. Copy retrieved May 1, 2009, from http://starbuck.net/node/30

Reed, H., & Van de Castle (1990). The Dream Helper Ceremony: A small group paradigm for transcendent ESP. *Theta*, Spring, 16 (1), 12-20. Copy retrieved May 1, 2009, from http://www.henryreed.com/reed/publications/dreamhelp.php

Rhine, L. E. (1981). *The invisible picture: A study of psychic experiences*. Jefferson, NC: McFarland & Co.

Rishel, K. A. (1998). Intuition and hypnosis. Unpublished doctoral dissertation, American Institute of Hypnotherapy. Copy retrieved May 1, 2009, from http://www.henryreed.com/reed/healingdreams/dreamhelpertranscript.php

Roberts, S. (2007). A story of a dream quest. *Intuitive-Connections Network*, February, 2007. Retrieved May 1, 2009, from http://www.intuitive-connections.net/2007/dreamquest-roberts.htm

Robertson, R. (2000). *Mining the soul: From the inside out*. York Beach, ME: Nicholas-Hays.

Robertson, R. (2009). *Indra's net: Alchemy and chaos theory as models for transformation*. Wheaton, IL: Quest Books.

Rossi, E. L. (2000). Exploring gene expression in sleep, dreams and hypnosis with the new DNA Microarray Technology: A call for clinical-experimental research. *Sleep and Hypnosis*, 2(1), 40-46.

Rossi, E. L. (2004). *Gene expression and brain plasticity in stroke rehabilitation: A personal memoir of mind-body healing dreams*. Retrieved May 1, from http://ernestrossi.com/ernestrossi/keypapers/PG GE PB Stroke.pdf

Schwartz-Salant, N. (1998). *The mystery of human relationship: Alchemy and the transformation of the self*. London: Routledge.

Schwartz, S. A. (2008). The beingness doctrine. *Explore*, 4(1), 15-17.

Smith, C., DeCicco, T., & Moran, C. (2009). Can individuals dream about the personal problems of others? Paper presented at the International Association for the Study of Dreams, Montreal.

Stearn, J. (1989) Edgar Cayce: *The sleeping prophet*. New York: Bantam.

Stein, M. (Ed.). (1995). *The interactive field in analysis*. Wilmette, IL: Chiron Publications.

Stevenson, I. (1970). *Telepathic Impressions*. Charlottesville, VA: University of Virginia Press.

Stolorow, R. D., Atwood, G. E., & Brandchaft, B. (Eds.). (1994). *The intersubjective perspective*. Northvale, NJ: Jason Aronson.

Stover, W. (2006). *Precognitive dreams for prosperity and abundance*. Retrieved May 1, 2009, from http://www.intuitive-connections.net/issue3/stover.htm

Tart, C.T. (1984). Acknowledging and dealing with the fear of psi. *Journal of the American Society of Psychical Research*, 78, 133-143.

Tart, C. T. (1986a). Attitudes toward strongly functioning psi: A preliminary survey. *Journal of the American Society for Psychical Research*, 80, 163-173.

Tart, C. T. (1986b). Psychics' fear of psychic powers. *The Journal of the American Society for Psychical Research*, 80, 279-292.

Thurston, M. (1978). Investigation of behavior and personality correlates of psi incorporating a humanistic research approach. (Doctoral dissertation, Humanistic Psychology Institute, San Francisco, CA, 1978).

Thurston, M. (1989). *How to interpret your dreams: Practical techniques based on the Edgar Cayce readings*. Virginia Beach, VA: A.R.E. Press.

Tick, E. (2001). *The practice of dream healing: Bringing ancient Greek mysteries into modern medicine*. Wheaton, IL: Quest Books.

Turrell, J., et al. (2007). *A life in Light*. Paris: Somogy Art Publishers.

Ullman, M., Krippner, S., & Vaughn, A. (1973). *Dream telepathy: Studies in Nocturnal ESP*. New York: Macmillan.

Van de Castle, R. L. (1994). *Our Dreaming Mind*. New York: Ballantine Books.

Van de Castle, R. L. (2004). *Response to 2004 IASD Lifetime Achievement Award*. Retrieved on May 1, 2009, from http://www.asdreams. org/lifetime/subidxlifetimeachievement.htm

Van Vliet, J. (2005). Healing from within. In Reed, H. *Dream solutions! Dream realizations: The original dream quest guidebook trailblazing intuitive dream guidance.* Rancho Mirage, CA: WePublishBooks, 45-48. Copy retrieved May 1, 2009, from http://www.intuitive-connections.net//issue1/healing.htm

Walsh (1996). *Will you dream for me? A qualitative study of the Dream Helper Ceremony.* Retrieved May 1, 2009, from http://www.henryreed.com/ reed/healingdreams/walsh1.php

Watts, R. (2002) *Dreaming for peace.* Unpublished essay. Retrieved May 1, 2009, from http://www. intuitive-connections.net/2004/dreampeace. htm

Webb, C. (2000). *Online Guest Interview on Dreams.* Retrieved May 1, 2009, from http:// www.dreams.ca/AOLchat2.htm

West, K. (1979). Dream Incubation for eyesight improvement. *Sundance: The Community Dream Journal, 3*(1), 91-97.

Wessling, N. Confessions of an experienced traveler. In Reed, H. *Dream solutions! Dream realizations: The original dream quest guidebook trailblazing intuitive dream guidance* (pp. 28-30). Rancho Mirage, CA: WePublishBooks. Copy retrieved May 1, 2009, from http://www.intuitive-connections.net/ issue3/wessling.htm

The Inner Voice
Amy I. Ramdass

Whispering of sad evenings
…and ruined mornings.
She tiptoes on soft feet
…never missing a beat

She warns of uneasy hours
…and moods turn dour
She adorns failed missions
…and ugly premonitions

She brings niggling doubts
…and fearful bouts
She sings of dreary gloom
…and impending doom

A hunch of something gone wrong
A chance to fix that broken song
She is dark and light
Your gift of inner sight…

Intuition is her name
Suspense is her game
She is your inner voice
Telling you to rejoice
…you have a choice.

For she's also a soft, summer breeze
…capable of putting your mind at ease

Amy I. Ramdass lives in Canada and works full time in the accounting field. In her spare time she blogs, writes novels and some poetry.
www.amyramdass.com

Lost and Found

Recovering Intuition for a World in Crisis

Matthew C. Bronson & Leslie Gray

Lost and Found

How do you find what was never lost?
Look where you are and then remember!
What can be known is already known-
Still echo, water, noise of leaves...
And—yes—the roses of late November.

The wind sliding against the ear
Admits the voices of singing ghosts.
Ancestral recitation of our prayer - for
Breath and life - from unseen hosts.

Particular noise? Molecules in motion?
Was it mockingbird taught you such,
To listen through colors of moving dawn
To lessons of the dusk?

Slim the thread, and slim the light
Joining Sky and Earth
And, just borrowed,
your thoughts and words-
From he who learned to heal while pained,
And she who heals with mirth.

At the unspecified time,
For the hour of deliverance
All souls assembled, expectant quake
To see the surging tidals break the
Mirror of forgetting waves
In shards of sweet remembrance.

Ecocidal Humanity

Matthew Bronson: Let's begin by addressing why people should care about or want to cultivate more intuition in their lives. For me, the essence is expressed in the opening poem: this is all about reclaiming what was actually never lost: activating a larger field of human possibility unblocked by background, culture or history. When we speak of intuition, we are not talking about something esoteric or suspiciously at the edges of the human project. Intuition is a natural part of us, part of our evolutionary heritage, part of who we are as human beings—but most of us have been systematically disconnected from it.

Leslie Gray: Well, we're so cut off from nature—and our own natures— that we're destroying our own life support systems. We are literally the only species on this earth that is destroying its own life support systems. I don't know of any other animal that does that. The other animals, for example, will not eat the plant that the insect it eats, eats. We on the other hand will cut down Amazonian forest to raise cattle and in the process destroy the very trees that enable us to breathe.

MB: I think we forgot somehow. And it's become so impersonalized that even global warming is an abstract concept. But maybe if it had a face on a poster staring back at all of us, you know, "Don't let the global climate monster steal our life breath!" or something. Maybe one of the reasons that we're at such a loss is that this is not a personal enemy. It's all of us together just going through our lives, and so the cause and effect relationship has been forgotten.

LG: Well, I mean it kind of does have a face when you see the polar bears disappearing and the icecaps melting in great shards. I mean, how much more of a face do you need to see?

MB: Most of our enemies throughout history have had a face, but now one can live a life that's quite comfortable, completely shielded from any disturbing images. Or if seeing those images, one can view them as exotic and far off and unconnected to oneself. There's nothing about the image per se that's going to mobilize me if I don't have some personal connection to it.[1] I'm saying that the work of social change

Matthew C. Bronson, Ph.D., see issue introduction for biographical information. **Leslie Gray**, Ph.D. practices psychotherapy in San Francisco, CA, and teaches ecopsychology and cross-cultural shamanism internationally. Her innovative work blending ancient and modern healing modalities has been featured in numerous periodicals including Shaman's Drum, Yoga Journal, East West Journal and in many book anthologies including Ecopsychology: Restoring the Earth, Healing the Mind and Original Instructions: Indigenous Teachings for a Sustainable Future. Dr. Gray is Executive Director of Woodfish Institute (www.woodfish.org), an educational foundation which promotes sustainable ways of living informed by traditional knowledge. Dr. Gray created the "Woodfish Prize" which is awarded annually for a creative project focused on this mission. She is a member of the Society of Indian Psychologists and of the Milton Erickson Institute of the Bay Area.

has become harder because we're not set up to deal with things that are happening gradually. There's this way where you put a frog in a pot and gradually heat up the water and the frog doesn't notice till it's boiling and it is too late to hop out.

LG: Is it that we're not set up, or is it that we're not making choices that involve courage?

MB: Well, I think that rings true too because part of the courage is being willing to say, "This isn't working; I know that something is horribly wrong." And people are afraid of being the one who says, "I know something is horribly wrong. We can't go on like this." There is a way in which I think we're all complicit, that we drag each other down or we hold each other back because who wants to be the one to say that the party is over and that it's really as dire as it is? Then you're the Cassandra.

The Spirit of the Enlightenment

MB: And there are all of the ways that people who use intuition have been punished in a rationalistic culture: this is something that we could talk about too.

LG: Yes, punished. Not to say "put on the rack," not to say "tortured."

MB: So it's not an accident that people are queasy about some of these matters.

LG: But, again, this is recent. People who intuited things were highly valued up until just about 8,000 years ago, maybe even less. Humans have been agrarian for about 7,800 years, industrial for about 120 years, and cyber-technological for about-maybe 60 years.

MB: Well, I think a turning point was the so-called Enlightenment.

LG: Yes.

MB: In the 1600s Descartes and the Pope came to an important deal that shaped the history of Western science and medicine. Descartes had been moving along in his metaphysical speculations in parallel to his scientific inquiry in a way that was rather threatening to the church, and he needed bodies to continue his medical experiments.[2] The Church controlled the death-industrial complex including the disposition of

human remains. So there was an actual meeting between Descartes and the Pope. And they agreed that Descartes would get all the bodies he needed for his medical experiments if he stopped all of his metaphysical speculation. This was a moment in which the spirit literally went out of Western science. To this day, the "pure" disembodied reason of Descartes and its resultant materialism reign supreme.

There needs to be a wakeup call, a call to remember and reactivate all our conscious and unconscious resources, all our faculties, because of what we face now. The idiot lights are blinking on the dashboard of the planet. Pick your process - intuition or scientistic rationality, the incoming data are all converging on the same terrible reality: most of the systems that support the living planet are crashing owing to human action; life as we know and cherish it will end within a matter of decades if the present trajectory continues. So what does it take? Maybe you see your individual work with clients as a small step in that direction because certainly with clients, you're remaking the world. You're remaking their ability to be more fully present and connected with others around them. And you're reconnecting with nature.

LG: And more broadly, my writing, my trainings and workshops, my work with the Woodfish Institute[3] are all efforts to go beyond doing it "person by person" and do things on a larger scale. The Institute awards grants to projects based on collaboration between indigenous and Euro-American people in the Global North, projects that are mutually and reciprocally transformative and benefit both communities. For example, we recognized and supported an oral history book documenting the life of Rolling

Thunder, a collaboration of his grandson and the renowned psychologist-researcher Stanley Krippner.

Now What?

MB: Collectively, what do you think is being asked of us?

LG: All the talk about global calamity, economic collapse and environmental destruction is really, at its root, about an inner crisis.

MB: Indeed.

LG: And I don't know if there is a "collective" way, in the sense of rounding people up or joining something or having a messianic figure come along to save the day—but earthlings are going to have to return to integrity or it will not change. People are going to have to empathically identify with the earth or nothing will change. People are going to have to have compassion for themselves as individuals and not get lost in a tailspin of self-blame—so that they can access the energy to change things. People are going to have to overcome the despair that comes from the knowledge of what has happened, the knowledge of what we've done.

MB: So imagination and empathy?

LG: We don't lack the economic, legislative, technological and intellectual fixes that we need for this. We don't lack them. But we do lack the will. We lack the integrity. We lack the commitment first to ourselves, and then to one another. We lack the feeling that we're in this together.

MB: I think that when people hear a word like "intuition" and our readers may resonate with this, it becomes a repository for all of these better parts of themselves that have been lost or that they mourn for. That's why a special issue on intuition is necessary because it's so devalued. The term becomes a placeholder, a Rorschach, an inkblot that we can project onto. It seems to hold an

Intuition is a natural part of us, part of our evolutionary heritage, part of who we are as human beings—but most of us have been systematically disconnected from it.

---

[1] See Bronson (2009) for a discussion of the necessary conditions for learning and change to occur.
[2] See Perth (1997: 18) for a discussion of this event and its significance in the materialist turn in science and medicine.

[3] See http://www.wooodfish.org for more information on the projects and grants mentioned here.

answer to the antsiness, the vacuum, the hole that modern people feel inside of themselves. Maybe cultivating intuition is really cultivating a kind of wholeness or a reconnection.

LG: Or at least including intuition as an equal partner in ways of problem solving.

MB: Yes, definitely. And I think really good problem solvers recognize that. And they include processes for generating intuition, through brainstorming, or any of a number of ways of visioning in non-ordinary states.

LG: They're ashamed to talk about it. They need to come out of the closet.

Coming to Our Senses

MB: Times have changed. The hour is late. So—intuitive scientists and others—it's time for you to come out of your closets!

Intuition is such a personal process and can show up in multiple sensory modalities. My colleague Tom Condon was working with some expert psychics and intuitives for a while. Using the principles of neurolinguistic programming, he modeled their language and tried to understand how it was that they spoke about intuition and what this indicated about their underlying states of consciousness.[4] He found certain common features such as the use of a gazing surface (a crystal ball, for example) as a means of focusing attention, but there was tremendous variety in the sensory imagery that intuitives used to describe their experiences.

We all have our own personal ways of connecting with these intuitive parts of ourselves. And it may very well have to do with the personal learning style or preferred sensory mode of the individual. So, for visual people, their conscious mode is visual. The visual stream becomes the dominant and preferred representational mode for the rational self. And for many of these same people,

the intuitive side comes through as, say, a kinesthetic impulse, as a feeling, as something that's in a different underdeveloped, under-articulated representational mode. The neglected cognitive function tends to be where the intuition shines through. So we have language for intuition from all these levels. "I flashed on it. I saw the light. There was an insight." The metaphors of light, of shape, color, that's one way people have of accessing and talking about intuitive

Photo: Chris Lynch

knowing.

Then on an auditory level, people say things like, "I heard a voice. I heard a still, small voice that told me what to do." And one thing I'm inviting readers to think about is: how would they recognize the intuitive voice from all of the other voices that are in their heads? So part of developing intuition is attending to and distinguishing among all of these voices as well as proprioceptive bodily/sensory experiences with increasing discernment. It's about attending to these facets of inner life that are so easily neglected in the press of the day.

LG: A felt sense.

MB: A felt sense. So there are visual, auditory, kinesthetic modes of presentation. I wonder if you ever thought about it in these specific sensory terms, that for somebody who is very visual you would recommend a kinesthetic exercise, or is it just integrated in your practice?

LG: Well, that's one of the reasons I use ritual because ritual helps you come back to your senses. And many times I will do something with someone, like

make a medicine pouch, and at the end of it I'll say, how many of your senses were involved in doing this? They felt a piece of quartz. They folded a piece of leather. They smelled tobacco. They smelled sage. They heard the sound of coyote bones rattle in a little dish. I mean I deliberately engage all of the senses. I think we have to return to our senses, so I engage them all via ritual.

MB: It's like building in a redundancy then. So it's a very rich sensory field.

LG: My intention is to build in 360 degrees of sensory possibilities for the patient to get something important in case they aren't just getting it verbally.

Is Indigenous Mind Intuitive?

MB: Yes, that makes perfect sense. Would you say that the Native American worlds that you've traveled in that there is a different conception of what intuition is, or is it that they have many of the same ideas that we're talking about but they just don't label it as something separate? When they say "thinking," is it a more encompassing field that includes something that we'd call intuition?

LG: Yes.

MB: But I'm wondering if there are ways in which we invested in Western European culture are working really, really hard to recover something which is just so taken for granted in indigenous cultures that it's almost hard to even articulate. I remember talking with some Natives about telepathy and going on and on about this telepathic example and how mind-blowing it was. And they were like, "Well, that happens all the time. So what?" There was absolutely no "gee whiz factor" in this whole elaborate narrative of psychic attack that we were focusing on in the conference. Some of the white people were tripping out, "Oh, wow!" and "Oh, what a coincidence!... And then you met the man who was telepathically attacking you in the Benares train station!" And the Natives were... unimpressed.

[4] The synthesis of Condon's research is available in an intuition training series that is excellent. Information about it can be accessed at http://www.thechangeworks.com/cwproducts/intuition-series.html

LG: Where was this?

MB: This was at one of the SEED dialogs.[5] We were trying to do something called the quantum linguistics dialog. And it started with some narratives about a psychic attack that an attendee had experienced in India, then was deconstructed seriously by all concerned. But the Natives were just completely bored.

LG: (Laughter)

MB: And the white people were on the edge of their seats. So there is something in here for me about how we're working really, really hard to recover something that may not have been completely lost within the indigenous world.

LG: Right.

MB: Do you think that's the case?

LG: Yes, I do. That's why I employ so many indigenous methodologies.

MB: To help restore some of that balance?

LG: And to do it faster. I mean, you just said, working "really, really hard" to recover it. I find one works really, really hard when one tries to use the non-indigenous framework to recover meaning.

MB: Yes, because meaning is so far away. It's been systematically pulled out of the framework so that you really have to work hard to try to get it back. Whereas, somehow, a meaningful world where everything is connected, everything is vibrating, everything is immanent and alive—it seems like that's more of the indigenous mode.

LG: Yes, and of course, indigenous people, like everybody around the world are hugely impacted by...

MB: Globalization and colonization.

LG: The Westernization of everything. In 1971, before electronic devices took over, and before you could find a McDonald's Beijing and a Nile Hilton, Alan Watts said, "We are moving towards the total Los Angelization of the world."

MB: He was right. He saw that one coming.

LG: So when you're indigenous now, you're simultaneously in touch with things that the dominant cultures are not, but you're also very much...the crap is

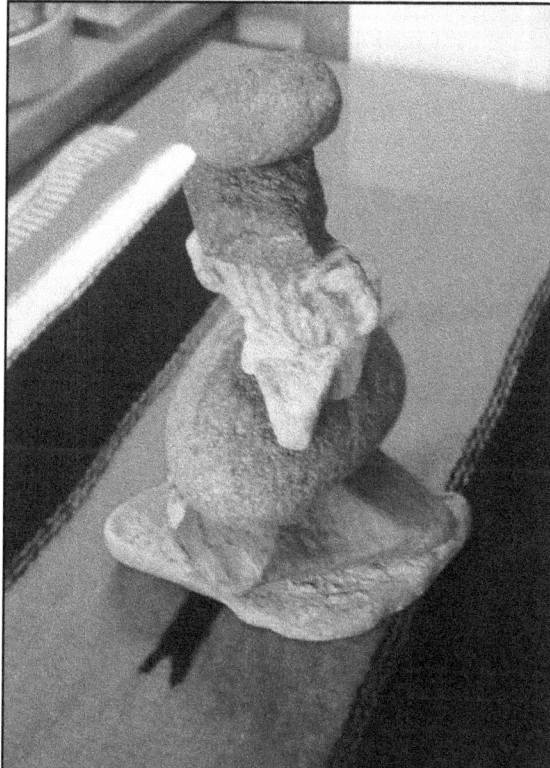

Photo: Chris Lynch

running downstream.

MB: You're talking about the most vulnerable, the poorest, the most precarious, the ones living in the most remote places, because that's the only reason that they haven't been completely colonized, it is because they're in some remote place. And maybe it didn't have anything that anybody found useful until suddenly they find that huge copper deposit under the sacred mountain.

LG: Yes, that's it.

MB: I get it. You're a hybrid. Indigenous life is a hybridization of these overlays.

LG: Yes, exactly.

MB: But I think this is also a wonderful opportunity. The dialogs we've been having in the Southwest among the Native American elders and scientists and so forth, these are an opportunity for people to tell their story and to be heard, if for no other reason than that the West, bless its lack of soul, is coming to terms with the fact that it can't go on any longer. In other words, it's been knocked down a peg. It's unfortunate that it took something like this. But I do see an opportunity for Native voices and for a revalorization of indigenous knowledge to occur.

You Lost Me at "Shaman"

LG: Do you really?

MB: I see the possibility. But I think it's been up to this point largely missed because it's been exoticized—the Pocahontas syndrome. Indigenous peoples are frozen in a fixed culture, frozen in time in the collective imagination.[6] The radical idea is advancing that indigenous people live and walk among us, and that these ideas and practices never died and are still current. I just see this becoming more generally accepted in the world. But maybe not from where you sit. In the course of your own career, if you were to measure the level of resistance to your work, you have to admit that it's not as hard now to do your work as it was before, right?

LG: In some ways it's not as hard and in some ways it's harder.

People who intuited things were highly valued up until just about 8,000 years ago

MB: It's harder?

LG: The ways in which it's harder is that before, in the 80's, I did not used to encounter people who were there to pseudo-philosophize about shamanism.

[5] Information about the annual SEED dialogs among native elders and scientists can be accessed at http://www.seedopenu.org/. For published discussion see Parry (2009), and the special double issue of *ReVision* devoted to the topic, "The Language of Spirit," Bronson (2004), also available as reprints directly from *ReVision*.

[6] See Bronson (2003) for a discussion of the exoticization of indigenous cultures with special attention to language extinction and revitalization.

I was mainly encountering people who actually were there to learn, and it was fun and something new. I had not yet encountered people who would take these ideas, dilute them and put them in publications that would lead people further away from experience than toward it. And because there has been so much abuse—the instant shaman workshops—I oddly end up catching the flack of people who have been operating that way.

MB: So all the people who have taken a few workshops and hang up their shingle as an authentic shaman despite a lack of mastery degrade the public perception?

LG: My interview in the magazine *The Sun* (Platek, 2009) was, I think, a serious attempt to address this. And I've had many people say to me that I was evenhanded, and indeed I consciously strove to be evenhanded. And yet I had a gentleman who is the head of some Indian organization write me that he simply turned off the second he heard the word "shaman." It didn't matter what I said, because of the word "shaman" itself. I've encountered a good deal of that.

MB: You lost me at "shaman."

LG: Yes, exactly.

MB: I understand.

LG: So that didn't used to happen.

MB: That's really kind of the blowback from cultural appropriation, from the way in which the word "shaman" has been appropriated, misused, distorted, is that right?

LG: Well, I suppose except that, yeah, not the term, but the actual appropriation of...

MB: Of the shamanic methods or practices.

LG: Right. What is easier now is that I don't have to explain myself so much. I don't have to give so many definitions. The popularization of shamanism has left me able to talk to even casual strangers on airplanes about it.

MB: Stories, all the back story about why your work is legitimate.

LG: Which I used to have to do copiously. In the 80's people would say, even if I said the word "shamanism," they'd go, "sha..what?" You know, like a total strange sounding word to them. That doesn't happen anymore.

MB: So at least it's in play, and you

have some beginning points. And I am just imagining what would happen if people who took like a weekend workshop in Catholicism started setting up their own Catholic churches, and how the Church would feel about that. Shamanism is not, could never be, an organized religion, but that means that you don't have central quality control. And, thankfully, you don't have an office of the Grand Inquisitor to kind of keep these things in order. So it's anarchy. It's just anything goes.

LG: Yes, it is true that the dilemma of a lot of native ways is that they haven't been codified and written in books and therefore can't be guarded. But on the other hand, they wouldn't be what they are if they had been written down like sutras or like the Bible or Koran, etc.

MB: That's how I understand the predicament. It wouldn't be about codifying it all, because then you're just putting another nail on the coffin of thought and spontaneity.

> The idiot lights are blinking on the dashboard of the planet. Pick your process – intuition or scientistic rationality, the incoming data are all converging on the same terrible reality.

Cultivating Intuition

MB: I wanted to ask you if you had some ideas for people about cultivating intuition in their own lives. What are some things that work for your clients? You mentioned the use of ritual, so personal rituals, other kinds of rituals, shamanic soul retrieval. What are things that people can start doing to reconnect with these parts of themselves? We're acknowledging that we're all wound-

ed. We're acknowledging that we're all alienated, separated, disconnected pathologically from the web of life around us, and that intuition is one way of making a move back towards that connection. What works?

LG: I'd like to see people in urban areas walk their blocks and know their environments, see the urban trees. I'd like to see that happen but I don't see it happening. I'd like to see more ways for people to come together.

MB: Community?

LG: Yes, come together and talk about this as a dilemma. There are seminars and public forums that occasionally attempt to do this in the Bay Area and I attend them. But they're hardly noted for their diversity of input. As for individuals, I use non-typical ways of having them increase their dreaming and paying more attention to dreams. That helps a lot.

MB: So you get them to really start paying attention and connecting with what otherwise was just this irrelevant thing that happened at night?

LG: We live in an over-psychologized society, and the only way that most people know of working with dreams is analysis and interpretation. And I get them to respect the dream world in and of its own as a world.

MB: You take more of a shamanic stance.

LG: Yes.

MB: Don't try to explain it.

LG: Yes, as they engage the figures in the dream rather than the purpose or...

MB: Explain them or interpret them.

LG: Explain them or explain them away, which is also what happens. I get them to act out parts of their dreams in their lives. It's active engagement.

MB: Do you have any specific meditation or mindfulness or other kinds of practices that you think can help? I mean you sometimes give people fetishes (sacred animal figurines) or you ask them to work with rocks, for example.

That's a very intuitive process. Could you describe that?

LG: I teach people to work with a medicine wheel, which is composed of rocks, in a way that gives them answers to questions. I also have a technique whereby they obtain a small rock to represent each image from a healing dream. Then I have them balance the rocks on top of each other. They find, usually to their amazement, how very many ways you can configure those rocks and still achieve balance. Like this right here, I've been doing this for three years (balances several odd shaped rocks), and I still find new combinations. Here, I'll do one now. I have never put that white rock with the crevice on the top because I thought it would fall over.

MB: So you are taking some rocks that are different shapes and showing how they can be piled differently.

LG: I change the order of the pile every other day.

MB: It makes you think about things in a new way. It forces you to be creative.

LG: The core definition of healing from a Native American perspective is "restoration of balance." It's not static. Healing is continuing readjustment.

MB: It is "balancing."

LG: It is astonishing how we tend towards balance in the same way that the human body tends towards healing. Most things, if left alone, will heal sooner or later. They might heal faster if you had an antibiotic ointment. But most things left alone heal. It's what the body does until it becomes aged and dies. The body seeks balance. Intuition is an expression of that same tendency toward balance and is the equivalent of the healing impulse. By creatively rebalancing the rocks, I am activating my own creativity, my more-than-rational capacity for problem solving in a world that is constantly shifting.

MB: I remember there was a whole school of healing where you would say,

People are going to have to empathically identify with the earth or nothing will change.

"My body balances itself perfectly" as a kind of affirmation.[7]

LG: Oh, really. I never heard of that.

MB: It's something we did with cancer patients and people living with HIV. It was a very powerful affirmation that would evoke this tendency towards balance, homeostasis. And maybe what we're talking about with intuition is a reaching towards balance. And that's why it's going to be really, really different for different people. I'm just wondering if this word "intuition" is kind of a placeholder for a "reaching towards balance?"

LG: The word "intuition" comes from the past participle of the Latin verb "intuere," "to look upon." Interesting how the meaning has changed over time.

MB: It meant originally just paying attention, looking upon something and knowing it for what it was! But now it is, in the dominant view anyway, paying attention to something beyond "normal" rational, awareness. It is now opposed to "rationality," wherein an idealized sign in an abstract map of the world is elevated over the sensual, animate object itself and the search for invariant laws replaces a dialog with the fluid logic of nature.[8] That sounds like one of the roots of our current troubles.

LG: And "reason" and "rationalism" come from Latin "ratio" that translates simply as "reason or plan." So there was not originally the contrast we have now.

Confronting the Shame of Intuition

MB: Are there any thoughts that

---
[7] For information about Autogenics relaxation exercises, see http://www.rush.edu/rumc/page-1193858443095.html.
[8] For a lyrical historiography of the ascent of abstract rationalism and its association with literacy see Abram (1996). For a contrast between indigenous and western modes of reasoning and language structures see Alford (2009).

you'd like to share about this contrast and the challenge of valuing intuition in rationalistic culture?

LG: I feel so aware of how much pain has been caused by the shaming of intuition—the deep pain that people who exercise their intuition have been subject to. The cost has been huge, and I'm not even right now talking about the environment.

MB: I know, just the psychic and emotional challenges.

LG: Yes.

MB: Well, I'm thinking about how hard it is for folks that are more intuitively oriented in terms of where they're actually drawing their sustenance and their values and what makes them tick. It is so hard to be wired more that way in this digital society. We do such a violence to people who can't necessarily explain how they know what they know. Even though it might end up to be the very best solution in the room, because they don't have a story about why that's the best logical possibility, it gets discarded.

LG: And also people like you were speaking of earlier, the scientists who know that they are using intuition and then have to hide that and put it in acceptable terms ... that I guess their cost is they have to deaden themselves.

MB: Yes, but that's the conundrum

People are going to have to have compassion for themselves as individuals and not get lost in a tailspin of self-blame

I think for a lot of scientists because it comes down to choices. Phil Sakamoto, a NASA scientist, who is one of the people from the SEED science dialogs in Albuquerque, was talking about how he was a specialist in these equations that have to do with modeling the way fusion takes place. And the Defense folks were offering him really big bucks, six digits and seven digits, a condo and a nice new car to take all this powerful knowledge and to use it for modeling nuclear weapons. But he was doing this work because he was intuitively drawn to big questions, the nature of the universe, the stars and astronomy. But they came dangling goodies in front of him, trying to lead him to the shadow side of the practical application of his knowledge. So I think there is a tremendous amount of hurt and pain and delicacy, vulnerability, because reason has held the day for so long that intuition hasn't really had an advocate at this particular table, do you understand?

The Tyranny of Rationalism

LG: Let's not call it "reason." Let's call it "rationalism."

MB: Rationalism.

LG: I respect reason.

MB: I respect reason too. So let's say rationalism. Rationalism has been a big bully. And now it shows itself to have feet of clay because when push comes to shove, rational concepts like the free market dissipate into fluff and nothingness. And in fact, what we recognize is that what feels like solid reality is nothing other than reified ideology.

LG: Exactly, and a clear indication of that is that during the economic downturn the very people who have preached free market the most — bankers, hedge fund operators, etc. — demanded to be rescued by the government rather than let the free market work.

MB: Like, "Oh, help me. I'm a pitiful socialist subject who needs a nanny state to come and help me."

LG: Right, and these are the same people with contempt for "welfare mothers."

MB: This is not an even or a neutral struggle. But it's one where I think rationalism is vulnerable. And many will agree that it's time for some more robust thinking. Look at where we have ended up with rationalism in charge.[9] And when we're able to show that better thinking generates better results, then in a sense that prompts the current paradigm to shift. So I'm thinking about how they were struggling for a long time with how to create a soap dispenser that wouldn't spew soap all over the place.[10] And one of the designers of the design team was sitting watching a horse def-

ecate one day. And he noticed the way the membranes of the horse's anus separated as it did its business and then kind of came back together and it was all very clean and efficient. And that became the basis for all liquid soap dispensers. It's based on the membrane of the way that the horse's anus was designed.

LG: And it's bio-mimicry.

MB: It's bio-mimicry. So we're coming back to how the source of intuition may be something as simple as just paying attention to our own nature, paying attention to the nature around us, reconnecting, remembering like in the poem. And that what we're calling intuition is really nothing other than a mode of being human in relationship with a living world. And somehow we've had to create this word "intuition" to point back to something that we've lost. So that's the opportunity.

LG: Precisely.

MB: We wouldn't need special issues on intuition if somehow rationalism weren't constantly putting itself up as the be all and end all. Maybe it's because this cult of a certain kind of reasoning is very much identified with the scientism

Rationalism has been a big bully — and now it shows itself to have feet of clay.

that you mentioned before, the idea that there is a single right way to know the truth. It must work actively to suppress the antecedent modes of being it perceives as rivals. It presents itself as the single Procrustean bed against which all other methods must be measured. And it is probably the legacy of the Enlightenment, certainly the legacy of colonialism that you have to push back all the superstition, all this dark nature. And also, I have to say, it has resulted in the violent and sustained suppression of the feminine.

LG: Well, it's also the legacy of the Inquisition too.

MB: No question about it. The image of torturing Nature on the rack until she revealed her secrets at the inception of the Enlightenment, was not merely a metaphor in its inception, nor has it been in many of its effects.

LG: Francis Bacon stated openly that the methods of the Inquisition informed his image of scientific inquiry.

MB: And at that time there were actual woodcuts to that effect and paintings. They really felt that one had to torture Nature to reveal her secrets (Merchant, 2008). So this antipathy between intuition and rationality is a really deep one. And I think if we're going to do justice to the topic, we have to acknowledge that these words have a history, a genealogy, that there is an ongoing struggle in Western history and culture between these different perspectives.

We're at a moment where rationalism is being reconsidered, this has been especially true since World War II. Up to that point, the master narrative of modernity was, "We've figured out the world, we understand our place in it, we're controlling nature."

The same ways of thinking were applied by the Nazis to the industrial scale destruction of human life. The subsequent reflection and soul-searching, originally Marxist in orientation, are the genesis of the Frankfurt school,[11] including Herbert Marcuse et al., as well as people like Viktor Frankl, and the early existentialists, and then Habermas and Michel Foucault. These thinkers were saying, "Well, if we had this all figured out with positivistic reason, and it was all so perfect, and this really was the right project, where did we go wrong?" And I think that's been a very powerful and an important intervention in the cult of rationalism.

LG: Or not only, "Where did we go wrong? ... Did we really have it figured out with reason?"

MB: That's the rest of it, the examination of how power creates knowledge rather than vice versa. As a result of this rethinking, inter-subjective dialog, con-

---

[9] For an in-depth critique of reductive rationalism and the corresponding impoverishment of human possibilities see Bronson and Gangadean (2006, 2009); Gangadean and Bronson (2004); Zajonc (2006).

[10] Gordon (1961) describes "synectics," a set of strategies for solving problems based on bio-mimicry and collaborative creativity.

[11] Martin (1996) provides a comprehensive account of the Frankfurt school and their impact on western thought.

tention and consensus become the bases of truth claims rather than some external, objective measure. Yet, how does this help us now?

There is some fair amount of rearrangement of the deck chairs on the Titanic: everyone is ready to debate which "policy" will save us. But the people who really get it understand that the underlying Western and industrial paradigm is literally running out of gas.

LG: Yes, but it's interesting. It happened just a few moments after the communist paradigm ran out of gas too.

MB: Yes.

LG: Both systems.

MB: The other had its own supposedly competing vision of "scientific socialism" but perhaps it was not so different in its reliance on a certain kind of reasoning and worldview. If reason, pure reason, and a rational and scientistic approach is what's gotten us to where we are, then clearly we need something very, very different because the same old thinking is not going to bring us anywhere new. Freud brought us that insight that insanity is to keep doing the same thing over and over and expecting a different result.

Shaming Intuition

And I wonder if we might turn to the history of science a bit, because the funny thing about it is that the people who are the most hardcore about science being a search for absolute truth are not themselves scientists. There is a way in which people who are outside the realm of science try to turn it into some sort of strategy for truth, a story for controlling people and keeping them in their places.

LG: Because they want to use it politically.

MB: Yes, to use it for some kind of a political agenda, whereas the scientists that I know, every single one of them admits that their best insights do not come from a process of pure reason. They come when they're walking the dog, when they're swimming naked in the ocean and suddenly they have a flash. There is the famous case of Kekulé and how the recognition that organic molecules were shaped in the benzene ring came to him in a dream as the

Worm Ouroboros, the archetypal image of intertwined snakes.

I'm an acquaintance with a Nobel Prize winner, Brian Josephson, who discovered the Josephson Junction, which is the basis of integrated circuits. He talks openly about how he has had many insights come to him in an intuitive state that he was later able to confirm with mathematics. When they write it up for the journals, they make it as explicit as possible and all of the real sources of inspiration and the intuition are expunged.

LG: They're forced to.

MB: They clean it up.

LG: They fear not having their work accepted by prestigious journals and they fear being ridiculed by colleagues.

MB: So talk to me about that. What's up with this intuition shame? My take on it is that it's mostly a middle manage-

The source of intuition may be something as simple as just paying attention to our own nature, paying attention to the nature around us.

ment problem. But, I just wonder, if it has to do with the construction of professional identity, what do we make of that?

LG: Well, the shame of intuition came about when it was relegated to the feminine, then the shame is the shame of being considered female, "unmanly."

MB: Yes, with all the witches and gay people being burned.

LG: It's the shame of identifying in any way with someone that's been victimized. "Women's intuition" is, by definition, a lesser way of knowing.

MB: Because of the testosterone-driven discourse around what's true! If I admit to you that I know something that feels really true to me but I can't explain to you how I know it in rational terms, then it's not admissible in the court of truth. It's not evidence. It doesn't count

for anything. It is not "oral history," it is "anecdotal."

LG: In the "court of truth," the judge is a man.

MB: And yet what's exciting is this is changing and shifting. Because of this crisis, it all feels like it's up to grabs. I mean I see a retrenchment certainly of more traditional people who are trying to say, "We've got to get back to some basic truths."

LG: Even Far Right people are sort of saying, "Well, I'm willing to go down with the ship, but I'm not even convinced myself anymore that anybody else is going to be on it with me because who is it going to be, the women, the Latinos, the gays?" I mean, by the time you count up all of the people that have been left out by this monochromatic group that has controlled things for so long, there's almost nobody left.

MB: That's what it's come down to: it's becoming a party of one. So the question becomes, what is this other movement, this reevaluation of all that's been left out?

So you're using intuition, I assume all the time. Maybe it's so integrated into the way that you work that you don't think of it as intuition. Maybe you could speak about the kinds of clients that you're seeing and how they get cut off from their intuition.

LG: Well, I get a lot of people who after the first session want to become a client because they see I get it that they are locked into or trapped within a linear way of being. And I get it that even though they "want out" they simply can't stop themselves. It's a habit. So I begin by joining them in this habitual way of speaking and then I gradually abandon it and shift into non-linear conceptions. And it's often rather funny while it's happening and we both laugh. Then I'll say, "Do you know there's an entirely other way to problem solve that is both more effective and more fun?" This approach would not work if they thought of me as someone who doesn't engage in logical linear sequential reasoning because I'm not any good at it.

MB: Right, so you kind of enter into their rationalistic framework, establish rapport with it and then deconstruct it to help it shift into something else.

LG: Yes, exactly. And they delight in

seeing that there is a playful aspect to non-linear problem solving.

MB: You must often need to derail the linear mind to get people in touch with a more intuitive way of being and knowing. Can you give an example of how you do that?

My work is one of helping people to remember what was never really forgotten.

LG: Sometimes I'll get someone who'll say, "I was trying to journey, but I'd slip out of it because I'd find myself wondering, 'Is this really happening or am I making it happen?'" And then, I will say to them, "Well, in the entire history of Western philosophy no one has been able to answer that question about ordinary reality. So why are you holding non-ordinary reality to an even higher standard than ordinary reality?" I'll say, "Tell me about your ordinary life. Is that happening to you or are you making it happen?" And they never can answer that. So I say, "Then why are you expecting to know that about non-ordinary reality?"

MB: So are you going for a shift of the focus from "Is it real or not?" to "How would you know?" because those are imponderable and a direct link to unending inquiry? You ask rather, "What good is it? Has it helped you? Was the information useful?"

LG: Well, that's what I tend to say. I say, "Why don't we just become radical empiricists and see what works rather than pondering whether or not something is 'real'?" I'll give them examples. I'll say, "Okay, is this real (knocking on mantle)?" And a lot of times people say, yes. I'll say, "Well what is it?" They'll say, "It's a mantle over a fireplace." I say, "Well, is it solid? Are you saying it's real because it's solid?" They'll say, "Well, yeah." I'll say, "You know, if we look at this with an electron microscope we can see that it's not solid at all, that it's moving constantly. And there is as much or more distance between the molecules in this object proportionally as there is between stars in space. And I sometimes invite them to envision the mantle through time-lapse photography. "See this mantle, now roll time back

and see it when it was a tree. Now to the future where it's laying in a garbage heap somewhere, and then it goes back into the earth. And now cabbages are growing out of it. So is it real because it's permanent?"

MB: And how does that question become an intervention for people?

LG: Well, I use it so that they stop going around and around in their head about whether or not they're "really experiencing" something. It's just the wrong question to be asking in the context of intuitive problem solving.

LG: But also you asked me something very specific. You asked me for examples of the contradictions in linear thinking. And those are several examples.

MB: Those are wonderful examples. It would almost be what Derrida talked about as deconstruction, which involves inhabiting the worldview of another and then via a reductio ad absurdum, taking what they're saying as a given and then just showing that what they thought was so substantial and important is not so substantial. You have shown how there are in fact some fixed attitudes we need to lose, if we are to come back to our senses.

LG: It is also a reconstruction. For healing to occur, there are experiences, attitudes and modes of being that need to be revalued and remembered once the trance of the everyday is interrupted. My work is one of helping people to remember what was never really forgotten.

References

Abram, D. (1996). *The spell of the sensuous: Perception and language in a more-than-human world.* New York: Vintage Books.

Alford, D. K. H. (2009). Manifesting worldviews in grammar. In M. C. Bronson & T.R. Fields (Eds.), *So what? Now what? The anthropology of consciousness responds to a world in crisis* (pp. 288-307). Newcastle-upon-Tyne, UK: Cambridge Scholars Press.

Bronson, M. C. (2009). The grammar of transformation: What ESL students can teach the anthropology of consciousness. In M.C. Bronson & T.R. Fields (Eds.). *So what? Now what? The anthropology of consciousness responds to a world in crisis* (pp. 232-253).

Newcastle-upon-Tyne, UK: Cambridge Scholars Press.

Bronson, M. C. (Ed.). (2004). [Special double issue]. Language of Spirituality, *ReVision, 26*(3-4).

Bronson, M. C. (2003). Rekindling the flutes of fire: Why indigenous languages matter to humanity. *ReVision, 25*(4), 5-10.

Bronson M. C., & Gangadean, A. (2009, in press). Encountering the (W)hole: Integral education as deep dialogue and cultural medicine, in S. Esbjörn-Hargens, J. Reams, and O. Gunnlaugson. (Eds.), *Integral education: Exploring multiple perspectives in the classroom.* Albany, NY: SUNY Press.

Bronson, M.C., & Gangadean, A. (2006). ((Circling)) the /square/: Reframing integral education discourse through deep dialogue. *ReVision, 28*(3), 36-47.

Bronson, M.C. and Fields, T.R. (Eds.). (2009). *So what? Now what? The anthropology of consciousness responds to a world in crisis.* Cambridge Scholars Press, UK: Newcastle-upon-Tyne. Book Web site: http://www.sowhatnowwhat.net.

Gangadean, A., & Bronson, M. C., (2004). The quest for a global grammar, mythos and cosmology, *ReVision, 26*(3), 39-48.

Gordon, W.J. (1961). *Synectics.* New York: Harper & Row.

Martin, J. (1996). *The dialectical imagination: A history of the Frankfurt School and the Institute for Social Research 1923-1950.* Berkeley: University of California Press.

Merchant, C. (2008). Secrets of nature: The Bacon debates revisited. *Journal of the History of Ideas, 69*(1), 147-162.

Platek, B. The good red road: Leslie Gray on rediscovering America's oldest psychology. *The Sun,* April 2009, 4-12.

Parry, G. (2008). *SEED Graduate Institute: An original model of transdisciplinary education informed by indigenous ways of knowing and dialogue.* (Unpublished Ph.D. dissertation. California Institute of Integral Studies, 2008).

Pert, C. (1997). *Molecules of Emotion.* New York: Simon & Schuster.

Zajonc, A. (2006). Cognitive affective dimensions in teaching and learning: The relation between love and knowledge. *Journal of Cognitive Affective Learning, 3*(1), 1-9.

THE 27TH INTERNATIONAL CONFERENCE
OF THE SOCIETY FOR THE STUDY OF SHAMANISM,
HEALING, AND TRANSFORMATION

WISDOM OF OUR ANCESTORS

BRIDGE TO THE FUTURE

SEPTEMBER 4-6, 2010
LABOR DAY WEEKEND
SANTA SABINA RETREAT CENTER, SAN RAFAEL, CA

An opportunity to engage with shamans, healers, scientists, anthropologists, medical doctors, psychologists, and artists and to explore new directions of cross-cultural healing in the 21st century.

For more information and to register, visit our webpage:
www.shamanismconference.org

The Third Ventricle

Temple of the Soul

Joyce A. Kovelman & Hoang Van Duc

This paper integrates findings of Eastern and Western science into a greater vision of self, world, and reality, and offers an expanded map and cosmology for such realization. In particular, we call attention to the brain's ventricular system which nourishes, supports and protects our Central Nervous System (CNS). We disclose a hidden purpose of the Third Ventricle, and provide evidence for its critical role in enabling humanity to attain higher states of consciousness.

Eastern mystics tell us that the mind is humanity's soul essence, which dwells within each of our hearts. But, ancient visionaries spoke of two very different hearts, not just one. The first, part of

Joyce A. Kovelman, Ph.D., Ph.D. explores the interface among psychology, science and spiritual traditions. She is impressed with the depth and scope of Wilber's integral model, and interested in the study of non-ordinary states of consciousness. Dr. Kovelman is a psychologist, scientist, international speaker, guest on T.V. and radio, and serves as an official ECOSOC representative to the United Nations on behalf of the Institute of Global Education. Her Web site is www.essentialsforasoul.com Rev. **Hoang Van Duc**, M.D. was born and raised in Vietnam, and is a life-long practitioner of Vo-Vi Meditation. After emigrating to the United States, he worked at The Rand Corporation in Santa Monica, and later at U.S.C. Keck School of Medicine in Los Angeles, California where he taught Attitudinal Medicine. Together with Dr. Zea of Beijing, the two scientists reconfirmed Eastern science's claim that the Third Ventricle is located in the exact center of the human brain.

our cardiovascular system, is found in the chest of each individual. The Eastern traditions refer to this organ as the bleeding, beating heart. Western science is also familiar with our physical heart. However, the manifest heart is not the same as the "True Heart" that mystics tell us can only be approached through the brain's Third Ventricle (H. Van Duc, personal communication, 1998).

The strategically located Third Ventricle dwells beneath the higher centers of cognition in the cerebral cortex, and above the more vegetative, housekeeping and survival centers of the lower reptilian brain (See Fig1). The Pituitary (master) gland and the Pineal gland surround and protect the Third Ventricle, leading some Hindu sages to refer to the Third Ventricle as the "Cave of Brahma." The centrality and depth of the Third Ventricle reflects its importance as well as its putative role as a portal to invisible, hidden and rarified realms beyond our five senses.

The concept of stages of development, with each level or stream influencing all other levels, creates a nested, interpenetrating holarchy of awareness and perception recognized by the ancient Eastern spiritual traditions and includes: the Seven Chakras of the Yogic traditions, the Ten Sephirot in Jewish mysticism, the Seven Gardens of the Alam-

al-mithal in the Sufi tradition, Dante's levels of purgatory, the Three Worlds of the Shaman, and the Great Chain of Being, (Kovelman, 1998). Wilber's (2006) 6-AQAL Integral Model, Kohlberg's stages of morality and ethical behavior, and Beck and Cowan's (2001) "Spiral Dynamics Integral," (based upon the research of the late Claire Graves, Ph.D.) have introduced postmodern versions of the various stages of psychological development.

MacLean's Triune Brain

Western science sub-divides the human brain into various systems and regions. MacLean's model of the "Triune brain" (Restak, 1984) reveals that our CNS system has three distinct, yet closely connected "brains" reflecting humanity's early relationships to both reptiles and mammals. MacLean tells us that each of the three arise during different stages of neural development. Moreover, each "brain" subserves very different functions and activities (See Fig. 1). For example, the reptilian brain of the archicortex is the first to develop, and is responsible for housekeeping, vegetative and autonomic functions such as breathing, heart rate, and response to threat and aggression. The second, the "Limbic" brain (paleomammalian) is essentially the emotional brain, which

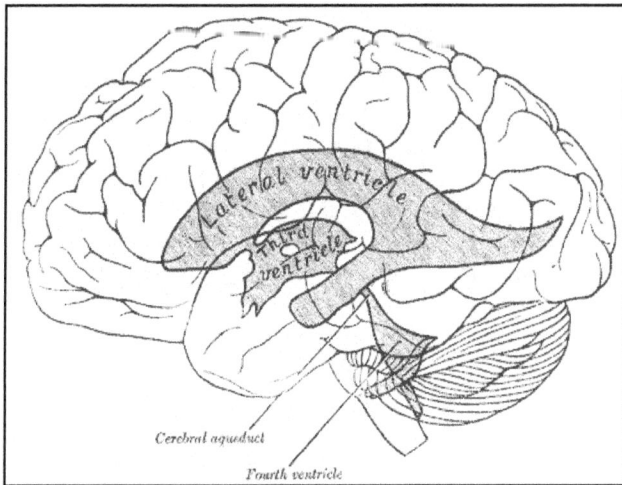

Figure 1. McLean's triune brain revisited and the four brain ventricles. This reveals the entire Ventricular System of the brain and its relationship to McLean's Triune Brain. The first brain is the archicortex or reptilian Brain and houses the Fourth Ventricle. It deals with the physiology and functions of the body. The second brain is the Limbic Brain (also known as paleo-mammalian), which houses the Third Ventricle and deals with discernment, emotions, feelings, altered states of consciousness, intuition, meditation, subjective mind and other ways of knowing. The third brain is the most recently evolved cerebral/neomammalian cortex that contains the 2 lateral ventricles, and is concerned with information, cognition, objective reality and logic (left brain), as well as with spatial, musical and artistic information (right brain) i.e. mind. Essentially, the Third Ventricle connects Heaven and Earth and serves as a gateway to Soul and Spirit. Hence, the four ventricles together integrate Mind, Body, Spirit and Soul, providing a satisfying wholeness to self and humanity. (Graphic: Gray's Anatomy)

exquisitely reflects who we are in the deepest core of our being. The limbic system also interacts with the higher cortical systems of the brain, ensuring that our feelings and perceptions are elegantly and faithfully translated into the many complex experiences and events of daily life. It is the limbic system that transforms our thoughts, beliefs and feelings into the molecules of love, hate, joy and fear, whereas the orchestration of basic needs, emotions, and perceptions takes place in the cerebral cortex (neomammalian). Regions of the cerebral cortex are involved in the highest levels of cognition and learning that Western science recognizes (Parent, 1996; Snell, 2001). In contrast, the Eastern traditions claim that the highest stages of learning and enlightenment take place within the depths of the Third Ventricle of the limbic, paleomammalian brain (H. Van Duc, personal communication, May, 1999).

Consciousness: Primary or Secondary?

An important difference between Eastern and Western understanding of the brain concerns the concept of consciousness. Most spiritual traditions insist that

consciousness is primary and exists necessarily. In fact, these ancient traditions claim that consciousness gives rise to matter, not the other way around. In contrast, Western science claims that matter is the source of consciousness, arising at birth and ending upon death. No more dissimilar cosmologies exist. It has led to tension and conflict between the two sciences (Kovelman, 1998).

The following quote indicates that some members of Western science are beginning to recognize the role of consciousness in creating our world, and in accord with Eastern scientists and ancient spiritual traditions, biocentric theory also seems to be approaching the idea that Consciousness is Primary. ".... we propose a biocentric picture of reality. From this point of view, life - particularly consciousness - creates the universe, and the universe could not exist without us" (Lanza & Berman, 2009, p.54). Although some scientists are beginning to recognize that Consciousness is primary, few recognize or explore the physiology of transcendence.

The Brain's Ventricular System

The brain's ventricular system is a vast reservoir filled with CSF (cerebrospinal fluid) that bathes and embraces the entire CNS (see Figs. 1 and 2). CSF is produced by the Choroid Plexus, a thin sheet of tissue found only in each of the four ventricles that make up this system. CSF prevents the brain from collapsing upon itself, as well as from harm due

to impact or injury (Parent, 1996; Snell, 2001).

"There is passage of water, gases and lipid-soluble substances from the blood to the cerebrospinal fluid. Macro molecules such as proteins and most hexoses other than glucose are unable to enter the cerebrospinal fluid. It has been suggested that a barrier similar to the blood-brain barrier exists in the choroid plexuses... It is probable that the tight junctions between the choroidal epithelial cells serve as the barrier." (Snell, 2001, p. 463.)

The Third Ventricle

The Third Ventricle lies deep in the center of the brain, where it integrates information from the cognitive, thinking aspects of the cerebral cortex with the emotions of the limbic system, as well as the autonomic housekeeping functions of the reptilian brain stem. (refer to Figs. 1 and 2, above). Essentially, our Third Ventricle connects mind, body and spirit, ensuring that we become more whole and aware. How we live, think, and believe determines whether we can

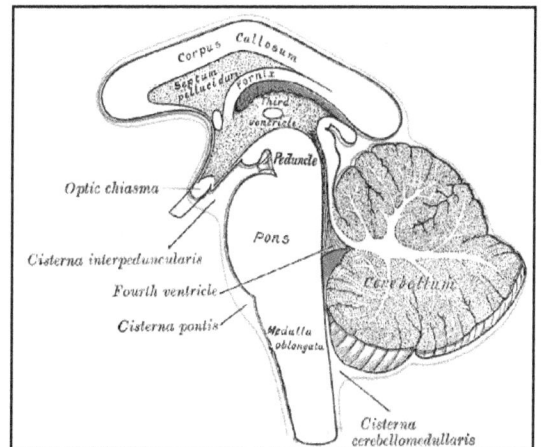

Figure 2. Saggital section of brain that reveals midbrain and brain stem locations of 3rd and 4th Ventricles

Graphic: Gray's Anatomy

live in harmony with nature and with one another. In 1980, Van Duc re-confirmed the claims of Eastern scientists and mystics when he was able to verify the extraordinary location of the Third Ventricle behind the 6th chakra known as the Third Eye, and directly beneath the Crown Chakra (see Fig. 3).

A person's feelings of love, hate, joy or sadness arise moment to moment, and are quickly translated into molecules of emotion that are effortlessly carried upon waves of CSF as it leaves the Third Ventricle to flow over the inner and outer surfaces of the surrounding brain (Pert, 1997). As such, the spiritual "True Heart" together with the body's beating heart not only keeps us alive; but also provides the opportunity to connect with the deeper recesses and dimensions of soul.

The Third Ventricle is a biologically privileged organ as the brain is the first to receive newly oxygenated blood from the physical heart (Parent, 1996). It is likely that the winds of Chi, Prana, and Breath, along with the three energy bodies associated with the subtle, causal, and non-dual states of consciousness also affect the vibration of the CSF within the cerebral reservoirs. A Blood-CSF barrier prevents very large molecules such as proteins, drugs, neurotransmitters and blood elements from entering the CSF. In this way, CSF serves as an important line of defense and is one of the first places pathology of the CNS is revealed, e.g., protein in spinal tap, (Parent, 1996; Snell, 2001).

The Na+/K+ Exchange Pump

Reports of a Na+/K+ exchange pump within the Choroid Plexus lining the brain's ventricular system is of special interest. This pump allows a slightly higher concentration of Na+ ions to move into the Choroid Plexus, and a concomitant concentration of K + ions to move outward. The resulting concentration gradient of Na+ and K + ions further distinguishes CSF from serum and/or an ultra filtrate of blood plasma (Parent, 1996). As a consequence, the authors suggest that the Choroid Plexus is continually immersed in an electro-biochemical gradient similar to that experienced during depolarization of a neuron after threshold is reached, and an action potential (AP) is generated down the nerve's axon.

CSF is the purest and most rarefied of body fluids, containing only electrolytes and a few small molecules. Although CSF resembles an ultra filtrate of blood serum or plasma, the density of CSF is considerably lower, because, as stated above, it does not contain or transport cell elements or large proteins

as does the cardiovascular system, (Parent, 1996; Snell, 2001). Pure CSF interpenetrates and nourishes the entire CNS, thereby enabling us to open to a higher consciousness if we but choose. As Ventricular CSF flows over the brain, it creates a gradient/field effect that influences how the nervous system speaks to itself, thereby raising the possibility that the Third Ventricle and "True Heart" of the mystics mediate an as yet unrecognized role in intuition, healing, meditation, and other non-ordinary states (Figure 4).

In Eastern and Western science, the thoughts and feelings we generate, create an ever-changing reservoir of emotions and experiences that continually color and influence the events of daily life. It appears that the neuro-chemicals that give rise to the more negative feelings of grief, fear, anger, and worry have very different vibrations and locations in the brain than the feelings of love, joy, compassion and healing. Only in the last few years has Western psychology shown an interest in the positive emotions of the psyche that contribute to each person's sense of well being, contentment, self esteem, and improved state of health (Fredrickson, 2001; Patterson & Seligman, 2004). Ground-breaking research by Bruce Lipton, Ph.D. (2005) provides further support for the benefits of happiness, joy, and love.

A consequence of the Age of Enlight-

enment and Reason was humanity's descent into a Flatland world of "it and its," along with the demise of both interiority and subjectivity. Intuition, meditation, channeling, and other non-ordinary abilities that were once considered sacred gifts of the gods, suddenly lost their prestige and glory. Today, those who use their gifts of intuition are often ridiculed and thought to have serious neuropathology. Sadly, valuable information and possibilities are lost or never acted upon, often to the detriment of the individuals who would most benefit from such knowledge.

Let us begin by developing a larger contextual frame in which to consider and study meditation, intuition, healing as well as other non-ordinary phenomena. Do we really know where ideas are born, or where our dreams originate? Where are the subtle, causal, and non-dual domains found? Are they involved in intuition as well as meditation and contemplation? Can intuition be taught and cultivated? Do we even know whether intuition, meditation, clairvoyance, precognition and other non-ordinary phenomena are distinct multiple intelligences as is mathematics, morality, aesthetics, spirituality, and interpersonal skills (Helfrich, 2007).

It is noteworthy that His Holiness, the Dalai Lama, regularly speaks to a Tibetan Oracle, and uses the informa-

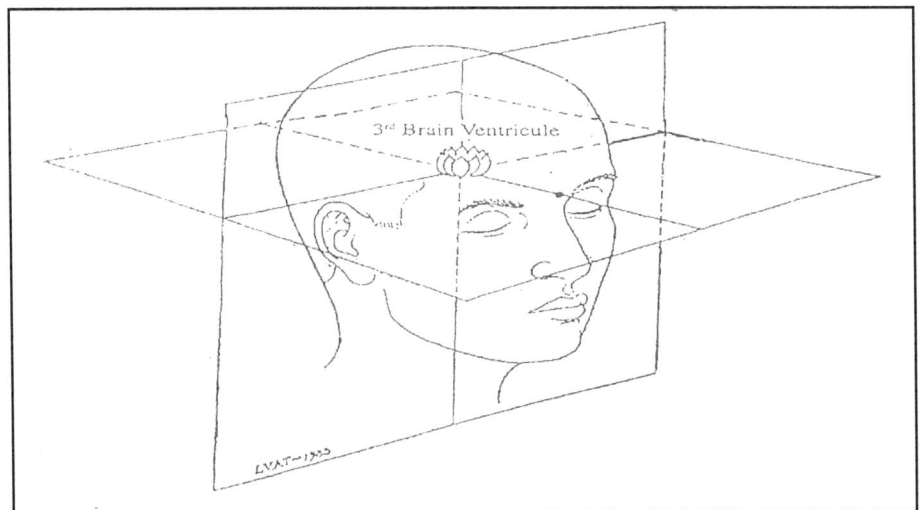

Figure 3. Temple of the Divine One. In 1980 Dr. Van Duc was seeking a new function for the Third Brain Ventricle suggested through his practice of Vo-Vi meditation-contemplation. He asked Dr. Zea, a Chinese scholar from Beijing, working in the Department of Radiology at USC, to determine whether the intersection of the two planes shown in Fig. 3 is or is not the location of the Third Brain Ventricle. The x-ray film was positive, revealing that the intersection of these two planes was the exact location of this mysterious organ. Dr. Van Duc's esoteric idea has been reconfirmed by science. (Graphic: Hoang Quy Luat, Liege, Belgium, 1983)

tion he receives to guide his actions and decisions as the spiritual Leader of the Tibetan people. Throughout his life, Carl Jung openly wrote about Philemon, his valued spiritual guide and teacher. The chemist Kekule` had an "ah-ha" experience that helped him discover the cyclic structure of the Benzene molecule following a dream he had of a snake biting its own tail. It was Kekule`'s discovery that opened the door to our present understanding of organic chemistry. Carolyn Myss and Edgar Cayce, two well known medical intuitives, have diagnosed illness in its earliest stages and often at a distance, to help patients heal and to stay well, much as shamans did in the ancient world. How can we show that the Third Ventricle is involved

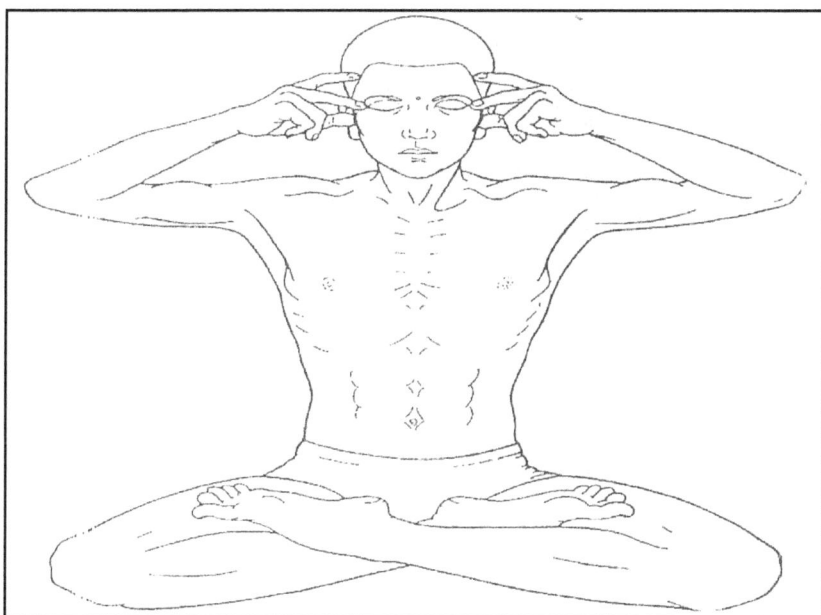

Figure 4. Meditation and Contemplation of the True Heart. (Graphic: Hoang Quy Luat,1983)

in intuition as the mystics claim? And why do some individuals seem to have a greater ability to receive intuitive information than others?

Intuition

We all know people who have had a 'gut' feeling not to fly on a particular day, and luckily listened to this warning. Only later did they learn that this plane crashed a few hours after take-off. And how many of us are willing to pay attention to our intuition when it reveals that it is not safe to drive on Tuesday due to impending danger? In this regard, Wilber (2006) tells us that most people who practice daily meditation for four or

more years attain one or two additional stages of development. We invite you to develop a daily practice of meditation and contemplation and encourage you to listen more deeply to your intuition.

Concluding Remarks

Although the ideas presented in this paper are provocative and of interest to many, some might ask "why" they should begin a daily meditation practice, and/or strive to enhance their intuitive abilities. Others may wonder whether the Third Brain Ventricle is really a gateway to more rarefied states of consciousness that can actually help us grow and realize our greater potential.

But Western science still believes that it knows all there is to know about the Third Ventricle. Currently, they are investigating non-local phenomena, the observer's role in determining which probable event will occur, the likelihood of multiple universes, and even study consciousness itself. Remarkably, many researchers are starting to "intuit" that their sudden insights, hunches, gut feelings, dreams, and unexpected "ah-has" are actually intuitive messages offering them vital information, clues and hints pertaining to their research designs, experiments and quest for new discoveries. In truth, scientific research depends as much upon intuition as it does upon the scientific method.

Fortunately, a deeper understanding

comes from Eastern sages and traditions who have long studied the Third Brain Ventricle ("True Heart") and its strategic relationship to the 6th and 7th Chakras. Their many studies of the Third Brain Ventricle have convinced Eastern scientists that exploration of these hidden, non-physical realms is not only possible, but necessary and beneficial to humankind.

Our "True Heart" invites us to travel where few have gone before. It is not by reading or talking "about" the journey that we grow and we evolve. It is only through our personal spiritual journeys that we enter into sacred space - allowing heart, mind and spirit to meet. Our journeys through and beyond our "True Heart" encourage us to explore the depths of our inner selfhood, a more peaceful humanity, and our awareness of what is. It is within these invisible realms of consciousness that we receive the lessons and possibilities most beneficial to our personal growth. As we evolve and transcend, we experience greater joy, more contentment, expanded intuition, and a deep, abiding love for all sentient life upon our planet.

Humankind presently stands at a dangerous precipice; the very survival of humanity awaits the choices we each make. Only a radical change of heart and mind can grant us the wisdom to heal ourselves and our world. Each of us is asked to become the change he/she wishes to experience in our world; each of us is invited to participate in a most extraordinary journey through time and space, and each of us is urged to visit the sacred realms beyond our physical world. When we pass through the gateway of the Third Brain Ventricle, we enter a space that fosters and encourages humanity's growth, evolution and transformation into a more noble species. Let us make it so!

My teachings are older than the world.
How can you grasp their meaning?
If you want to know me,
Look inside your heart.
(Mitchell, 1991).

References

Beck, D. & Cowan, C. (2001). *Spiral dynamics: Mastering values, leadership, and change.* Malden, MA: Blackwell.

Brodal, P. (1992). *The Central Nervous System: Structure and Function.* New York: Oxford University Press.

Fredrickson, B. (2001). Joy and love genetically encoded. *Research News and Opportunities in Science and Theology.* September, pp. 22-23.

Heimer, L. (1995). The human brain and spinal cord (1st ed). New York: Springer-Verlag.

Helfrich, P. M. (2007). The channeling phenomenon: A multi-methodological assessment. *JITP,* In Press.

Kovelman, J. A. (1998). *Once upon ASOUL: The story continues...science, psychology and the realms of spirit.* Carson, CA: Jalmar Press.

Lanza, R., & Berman, B. (2009). Biocentrism: How life and consciousness are the keys to understanding the true nature of the universe. *Discover: Science, Technology and the Future* (p.54).

Lipton, B. H. (2005). *Biology of Belief: Unleashing the power of consciousness and miracles.* Santa Rosa, CA: Mountain of Love/Elite Books.

MacLean, P. A. (1984). The triune brain. In R. Restak (Ed.), *The brain* (pp.136-137). New York: Bantam Books.

Mitchell, S. (1991). *Tao Te Ching.* New York: Harper Perennial.

Parent, A. (1996). *Carpenter's Human Neuroanatomy* (9th ed.). Quebec, Canada: Williams and Wilkins.

Patterson, C., & Seligman, M. (2004). *Character, strengths and virtues: A handbook and classification.* Washington, D. C: Oxford University Press.

Pert, C. (1997). *Molecules of emotion: The science behind mind-body medicine.* New York: Touchstone.

Snell, R. S. (2001). *Clinical neuroanatomy for medical students.* Baltimore: Lippincott Williams & Wilkins.

Van Duc, H. (1992). *Vo-Vi esoteric science* (M. Emoto, Ed.) (pp. 98).Tokyo: Japan.

Ventricular System. (2009). Retrieved June 1, 2009 from Wikipedia: http://en.wikipedia.org/wiki/Ventricular_system

Third Ventricle. (2009). Retrieved June 1, 2009 from Wikipedia: http://en.wikipedia.org/wiki/Third_ventricle

Wilber, K. (2006). *Integral Spirituality.* Boston: Shambhala.

Wilber, K. (2003). Excerpt B: The many ways we touch: Three principles helpful for any integrative approach. Retrieved June 1, 2009 from: http://wilber.shambhala.com/html/books/kosmos/excerptB/intro.cfm

Graphic Credits

Children's Poetry Facilitated by J. Ruth Gendler:

Your Soul's Eye

Alex Trux (At Age 8)

I see with the eye of the wind, and observe with eye of the breeze.
It really doesn't matter where I look,
for all I want to see is the wonderful works of Mother Nature.

My favorite place to see is in the cool shade
beneath the weeping willow,
while I calm her dreadful worries, and look up to see
bold, fierce pines towering above the sky.

When I look down, I see the rich black soil
and the amber leaves sitting peacefully by the galloping stream.

And when I look from side to side, I see
all the creatures of the forest,
the tough moose, the graceful doe,
the clever fox, the playful rabbit, and
the rapid squirrel.

But then I have to go into my horrible sealed bedroom
with blank walls and no imagination.

For the human race is doubtful,
and every single person thinks they have already set their hopes
and dreams, but really,
their only wish is to be free to see with their own eye.

J. Ruth Gendler is the author of *Notes on the Need for Beauty, Changing Light: The Eternal Cycle of Night & Day,* and *The Book of Qualities.* She teaches creative writing to children and adults. All examples in this issues are from her classes. On the web she can be found at www. redroom.com/author/j-ruth-gendler.

Integral Intuitive Communion With Gaia

Prabhath P

I ntuition is generally considered as the ability of an individual to gain knowledge and insights without the application of reason or logical analysis. It is widely accepted that intuition grasps knowledge in a holistic way unlike reason, which is reductionist and understands reality by analyzing the parts of a whole. People who have learned to access intuition, use it as an inner guide in their personal and professional lives. Intuition is also often equated with psychic abilities involving dreams, predictions and prophecies (Auerbach, 1999). Intuition plays a role in the creation of literary and scientific works, and in spiritual realization. But these perspectives of intuition, though not reductionist, still look at intuition in individualistic or particular contexts, without taking into account the larger wholes in which the human experience of intuition is embedded (Ferrer & Sherman, 2008).

The Indian yogi and integral philosopher Aurobindo (1997) offered insights into the multidimensional nature of intuition:

> Intuition has a fourfold power. A power of revelatory truth-seeing, a power of inspiration or truth-hearing, a power of truth-touch or immediate seizing of sig-

See issue introduction for biographical information on **Prabhath P**.

nificance, which is akin to the ordinary nature of its intervention in our mental intelligence, a power of true and automatic discrimination of the orderly and exact relation of truth to truth, these are the fourfold potencies of Intuition. Intuition can therefore perform all the action of reason, including the function of logical intelligence. (p. 949)

So integral intuition is not inimical to reason or logic, but reason can serve intuition by applying the intuitive insights for practical results.

Intuition has a deep spiritual significance. Intuition works across time and space and bestows upon us a deep understanding of ultimate reality as Satprem (1996), the disciple of Aurobindo, pointed out:

> Intuition reproduces, on our scale, the original mystery of a great Gaze: a mighty glance that has seen all, known all, and that delights at seeing bit by bit, slowly, successively, temporally, from myriad points of view, what It had once wholly embraced in a fraction of Eternity. (p.179)

According to the view being advanced here, a process of integral intuition involves going beyond the stage of disconnected intuitive flashes in order to access many interconnected dimensions of reality as a whole through an expanded consciousness. For example, a psychic focused on predictions may be focusing on accessing only the psychic aspect of intuition

to get flashes of relevant information. However, those who practice integral meditation methods may tune into other dimensions of consciousness also such as the human collective unconscious, the Gaia consciousness of Earth and the Transcendental Being. An example of this process can be seen later in this paper in the glimpse of the meditative experience of communion with Gaia consciousness from Integral Gaia Yoga, which I am developing.

The Living Earth

Before discussing how integral intuition can be applied for manifesting a conscious communion with Gaia, an exploration of the integral intuitive dimensions of Earth as a living organism is necessary. Here, a few representative Western scientific models that try to see Earth as a holistic entity are discussed. The scientist Lovelock (1979) proposed that Earth functions like a self-regulating system that includes the living beings of the biosphere, air, ocean and land of the planet and named it after Gaia, the Greek Goddess of Earth. Lovelock's concept of Gaia is a rationalized and scientific version of an ancient understanding of Earth. Many ancient cultures understood Earth as a sentient living being and even a superconscious Goddess with physical, psychic and spiritual dimensions. Capra (1996) has observed:

> The view of the Earth as being alive, of course, has a long tradition. Mythical images of the Earth mother are among the oldest in human religious history. Gaia, the Earth Goddess, was revered as the supreme deity in early, pre-Hellenic Greece. Earlier still, from the Neolithic through the Bronze Ages, the societies of 'Old Europe' worshipped numerous female deities as incarnations of Mother Earth. (p.22)

In India, Earth was worshipped as a Goddess named Bhoomi Devi. However, Lovelock, who formulated his theory within the confines of conventional scientific parameters, does not see Earth as a sentient living organism, but only as a self-regulating system without any teleological element.

The awareness of the interconnected web of life on Earth was prevalent in ancient times. Many poets, philosophers and mystics have expressed their understanding of the interwovenness and interdependence of everything. The Buddhist teaching of Interdependent Co-Arising is, for example, similar in some aspects to the processes of the web of life. The essence of this basic Buddhist teaching is that "all psychological and physical phenomena (dharmas) that make up what we know as existence are interdependent and mutually condition each other" (Hanh & Neumann, 2006, p.87). Likewise, nothing on Earth exists as a separate entity. All beings of the Earth exist in a type of inter-being made of a complex web of dynamic interrelationships. This interconnectedness is deeply intuitive and spiritual too according to the famous exponent of practical intuition, Day (1996):

> If there is anything intuition demonstrates, it's the interconnectedness of everything....No two snowflakes are alike, but their ability to lay together in a communality creates a snowfall. It's through our intuition that we can explore not only our differences but our oneness. This search for connectedness - whether to our planet, to God, or to one another - is my definition of spirituality. (p.178)

Conventional scientific reductionism with its emphasis on the objective, quantitative, empirical and analytical approach of dissecting an interconnected whole into separate parts for understanding it, fails to fathom this deep interconnectedness that is physical, biological, intuitive and spiritual at the same time.

The very word "environment" is limited in scope, because it arises from an underlying assumption that the biosphere and the geographical or atmospheric aspects of Earth are all separate from the human species. This is an erroneous notion because we do not live on the surface of Gaia, but we are immersed in the

Tree of Life — Image: Prabhath P ©2004

All images used in this article rendered from original color versions to black and white for the purposes of publication.

Gaian web of life. Our existence itself depends on continuous interaction with the complex processes of this web of life though most people are not consciously aware of this immersion in the planetary consciousness. Abram (1984), the American cultural ecologist, in his famous and much-reprinted essay "The Perceptual Implications of Gaia," explored the profound implications of our immersion in Gaia. He explained that our existence inside the Earth's atmosphere is very important since we cannot exist without its support and nourishment. The

atmosphere is a dynamic extension and functioning organ of Earth. As active parts of Earth's atmosphere, we are circulating the breath of the planet through our bodies and brains. We are constantly exchanging vital gasses and chemical information with other living organisms. Gaia is a reality, a psychological, intuitive and organic presence that encompasses us.

Abram pointed out that the mechanical model of reality, based on the absolute separation of mind and matter, is obsolete. The understanding of Earth as Gaia, according to Abram, suggests an alternative view of perception: Perception is communication. He preferred the term "communion," which is more precise than "communication." "Communion" denotes a deeper mode of communication without words. Perception involves the whole play of the senses and it is a constant communion between ourselves and the living world that encompasses us. So our perception of reality and the universe beyond the planet is also colored by our immersion in the atmosphere and biosphere of Gaia. Abram explains that our environment made of myriad forms of human and nonhuman biotic experience constitutes a coherent global experience of life, which has its own sentience and creativity. This communion with Gaia is undoubtedly intuitive and more intense than any other form of communion. Abram asserted that Gaia can't be reduced to a mere formula. Gaia is our own body, our flesh and our blood. Gaia is also the wind blowing past our ears and the hawks wheeling overhead. Gaia can be understood with the senses and recognized from within as far vaster, far more mysterious and eternal than anything we may ever hope to fathom.

It is clear from Abram's insightful essay that humanity as a species is intimately connected in an intuitive communion with Gaia. However, the over-emphasis on reductionist rationalism and modern educational, social and economic systems based on a mechanical worldview has suppressed this awareness from emerging in our conscious minds.

Restoring the Communion with Earth

Global warming is a burning issue that is causing serious alarm and ideological conflict within human society (Houghton, 2004). Current environmentalist initiatives that try to tackle global warming by addressing the issue with mainly rational and scientific approaches, though useful, are not enough to reverse an impending ecological holocaust. Such approaches are inadequate to deal with the root causes of the crisis in an integral way. The ecological crisis we face now is not just a result of the "assault on reason" that Gore (2007) has highlighted.

It is also, more importantly, the result of a spiritual crisis of consciousness caused by the relentless assault on our deep intuitive connection with Earth. The dominating social, economic and scientific paradigms of the Industrial Society are anchored in a mechanical view of nature. The Industrial Society's obsession with economic profit and its ways separated from nature have resulted in elite sections of humanity exploiting the living Earth for unsustainable and ecologically damaging goals of a delusional material progress, leading to severe ecological disturbances. This makes the self-organizing systems of Earth initiate balancing measures to correct the imbalances. Global warming can be seen as a symptom of this complex process. The imbalance now seems to have reached a stage where it can be reversed and the ecological balance restored only if humanity proactively participates with the dynamic processes of Gaia to resolve the worsening damages unwise human activities have inflicted on the web of life.

Humanity needs to urgently explore all possible ways for reconnecting with the web of life to intensify the restoration

of the ailing health of the planetary systems. The ecopsychologist Cohen, who pioneered the Natural Attraction Ecology Model, has emphasized the significance of our intuitive connection with nature and has also developed some methods to restore humanity's lost intuitive communion with Earth (Cohen, 2008a). According to Cohen, all beings including the human species and everything in the natural web of life are connected through natural attraction senses. In us, 53 of these natural attraction senses register emotionally and spiritually. Before

A process of integral intuition involves going beyond the stage of disconnected intuitive flashes in order to access many interconnected dimensions of reality as a whole through an expanded consciousness.

humanity appeared on Earth, the natural world and its spirit, an attraction to support life-in-balance called green spirit, thrived. Garbage, pollution and war were unknown in those times when nature's self-correcting perfection and restorative powers existed without human interference. Unadulterated natural systems support, personal, social and ecological well-being. The 53 natural attraction senses are actually the manifestations of the green spirit. For example, our sense of thirst attracts us to drink water and sustains us through the global water cycle. These senses include our love of community, reason and trust; aroma, place and consciousness; color, taste and motion; belonging, beauty, music and gravity along with 40 additional natural sensory attractions.

Cohen's research revealed that our social, psychological and environmental disorders are triggered by the Industrial Society's prejudice against nature. This prejudice socializes us to drive the green spirit callings of the 53 natural senses out of our awareness into our subconscious where they remain injured and frustrated. Because the Industrial Society rejects the purifying gifts of natural systems,

the health of people and natural areas deteriorates. To fill the void produced in the human psyche due to the disconnection with the green spirit, the Industrial Society manufactures artificial substitutes and excessively exploits nature for profit and power. To correct this imbalance, Cohen created a hands-on nature-connecting sensitivity tool to eliminate our natural-sense deprivation. It is the accredited, nature-connected education, counseling and relationship building Natural Attraction Ecology Model, an Applied Ecopsychology, Ecotherapy and Environmental Education process. This was born out of his 30 years of all-season travel and study in over 260 national parks, forests and subcultures.

This process empowers individuals through moments that let Earth teach (Cohen, 2008b). It helps participants transform their ignorance and the deterioration of the web of life into mutually supportive relationships with its natural systems in the environment, other people and themselves. Participants in the nature-connection web of life activities of Cohen's Project NatureConnect reported that their separation from nature subsided when they genuinely connected their thinking with nature through webstrings. According to Cohen, webstrings are the interconnecting threads in nature that build and hold together the web of life. In his view, these webstrings are natural attractions that have operated from the beginning of time and are found in every, person, place and thing. He tried to demonstrate the existence and working of the webstrings through his web of life activity workshops. Most of his workshop participants were college or graduate students, professional educators, counselors and coaches.

Cohen was inspired by an environmental education activity he witnessed in 1972 in the Smokey Mountain National Park. In this activity, a group of park visitors including children, were placed in a circle and each person was given a card to wear. On each card, a part of nature was inscribed: bird, soil, water, tree, air, wolf etc. A large ball of string was used to demonstrate the interconnected relationships between things in nature. For example, the bird ate insects, so the string was unrolled and passed from the "bird person" through the hands of the "insect person." The string represented their connection. The insect lived in a flower. So the string was unrolled across the circle through the hands of the "flower person." The flower was supported by the soil. So the string continued across the circle through the hands of the "soil person."

In the activity, the ball of string became a web of strings (webstrings), which passed through the hands of the participants and interconnected all parts of nature with each other. The activity continued by asking the participants to gently lean away from the web they built while holding it. They sensed how this thin string peacefully united, supported and interconnected them and all of life.

To identify and explain the strings in the web of life, Cohen later modified this original web of life activity. In his version of the activity, he did not start the demonstration with the labeled cards. Instead, he started by asking participants to: 1) visit the natural area around them for five minutes, 2) find two or three things there that for at least five seconds they felt attracted to, 3) identify what they liked about these attractive natural things 4) return to the web of life circle. After returning, the participants wrote on a card that they later wore, one of the natural attractions they found and one that had not already been chosen by another person to ensure an optimum of diversity in the circle.

In this modified web of life activity, he added two participants to represent humanity.

An additional, singular red ribbon connected these two people in the circle. The ribbon represents how in the web of life, human beings alone connect with each other using the written or spoken abstractions of literacy, of our words and

stories. Cohen argues that the exclusive focus on our abstract, rational and linguistic stories about reality causes the disconnection from the non-verbal natural attraction energies of the webstrings, which communicate through ways that are not rational or linguistic. So he calls for a more inclusive focus that connects humanity to webstrings too.

In one of his later workshops, Cohen asked the participants to explore and express what they felt and sensed as part of the web of life. The participants had to do an activity to discover what the webstrings might be. They were asked to find any attractive object in a natural area, and push or pull it with their total energy without dislodging it from its attachment or moving it from its place. Through this activity, the participants sensed some of the attraction energies that connected things to each other and the whole web of life. They became aware that their felt-sense attractions to

things in nature were also webstrings and that these webstrings pulsated. As they changed every moment, they re-registered in the things they connected.

For example, if a person saw a bird and the bird saw the person, the bird might move and the person might move in return. This pulse would continue until other attractions called. Both the person and the bird registered and reacted to the in-balance webstring senses of motion, sight and distance and many others. The participants recognized that the webstrings were connective attractions

by all of life to get food, water, habitat, energy, minerals, warmth, community and support. They also realized that, in their psyche, these attractions were also senses or desires that they experienced like hunger, thirst, trust, belonging, respiration and place. They understood that human beings are also webstrings in action. They saw that every part of the global life community was part of the web and that everything consisted of, and was held together by webstring attractions. Webstrings naturally bonded things together in mutually supportive ways. While evaluating the web of life activity, most participants reported that the webstring activity helped them see that, in the web of life, some form of restorative and connective webstring energy produced, balanced and unified nature.

The webstring attraction senses registered in their consciousness as sensations and feelings. They also became aware that the substitute artificial satisfactions, which the Industrial Society produces to satisfy their nature-disconnection wants, did not have the renewing and balancing natural powers of webstrings. Instead these substitutes produced stressful side effects in natural systems, people and the environment. Cohen's nature-reconnecting activities enable participants to safely bring webstrings back into their lives and thinking. The presence of the self-correcting ways of webstrings helps them organically reinstate naturally balanced personal and environmental well-being. Though Cohen does not use the word intuition explicitly to explain the workings of his model, it is clear from the experiential process of his model that it involves accessing and applying aspects of integral intuition that intensely connect his students to the refreshing webstring energies of Gaia consciousness.

Technology in Tune with Gaia

Technology has become so pervasive in the human civilization that it is not

> **As active parts of Earth's atmosphere, we are circulating the breath of the planet through our bodies and brains. We are constantly exchanging vital gasses and chemical information with other living organisms. Gaia is a reality, a psychological, intuitive and organic presence that encompasses us.**

possible to remove all technological aspects. What needs to be questioned is not the existence of technology itself, but those technological applications, which follow the Industrial Society's mechanical model that harm the ecology and disrupt the human communion with Gaia. Technology if applied in an intuitive and Earth-friendly way can intensify the probabilities of enhancing human-

and co-creating with people who care for the Earth and work for a planetary consciousness.

The fascinating 3D virtual world Second Life (http://secondlife.com) is another intriguing technological invention that has put me in touch with the potential emergence of technology that is in tune with Gaia consciousness. Second Life is a complex, imaginative and cre-

from intuition, technological fundamentalism that tries to conquer Gaia will remain dominant. Some people see virtual worlds too as an escape from the planet and physical existence. This attitude shows the lack of an integral intuitive understanding. When we realize through integral intuition, the interconnectedness of everything, we will recognize that technology itself has its origin in the collective consciousness of Gaia, of which humanity is a part. This recognition can awaken humanity to the need for technology to be in tune with the planetary web of life. In such a scenario, technological infrastructure that does not increase the carbon footprint can be evolved to transform the internet or virtual worlds into yet another dimension of Gaia consciousness rather than something that disrupts Gaia's dynamic balance.

Gaia can be understood with the senses and recognized from within as far vaster, far more mysterious and eternal than anything we may ever hope to fathom.

ity's communion with Gaia. Any form of technology is like a double-edged sword. One example in this context is the internet. The World Wide Web is misused by many misguided elements for spreading crime, pornography, soulless commercialism, terrorism, religious fanaticism and what not. But the very fact that the internet makes it possible for people living in distant corners of the world to interact instantly, makes it a tool that can be helpful for promoting co-operation and co-creation between diverse sections of the human population. Social media like social networking sites and online discussion groups enable people from different countries to become friends and learn one another's culture and ways of thinking. This makes it easier for people to open themselves to the intuitive awareness that national boundaries are artificial and that we are all parts of the collective consciousness of the same planet Earth.

My online association with the Intuition Network (http://www.intuition.org), an international network that promotes the use of intuitive resources, happened after I joined their online discussion group. It is through my interaction within this intuitive discussion group that I came into contact with ReVision Journal itself. Such possibilities would have been impossible without the existence of the internet. My participation in social networking websites that focus on intuitive, spiritual and ecological concerns have helped me a lot in connecting

ative virtual reality world. The avatars of Second Life residents can fly, teleport to any location within the virtual world and shape-shift into any form. While conducting online introductory classes and interactive discussions on Integral Gaia Yoga in Second Life, I found that I can interact in real time with people from all over the world despite the participants logging in as avatars from vastly different geographical and time zones. This opportunity to connect, cutting across time and space, triggers in many people an intense intuitive experience of the interconnectedness of the web of life.

The 3D virtual worlds are already being hailed as the future of the internet. However, the evolution of such technological innovations can act as catalysts for increasing the awareness of our immersion in Gaia only if we take an integral intuitive path that values the intuitive evolution of consciousness. When technological evolution is controlled by those who are disconnected

If artificial intelligence researchers discard their linear materialistic approach and allow the intuitive realization that Earth and the Cosmos are living organisms, they could possibly create an artificial intelligence program that learns to be intuitive by interacting with the meditative and intuitive consciousness of people through virtual worlds. It is not impossible that such an artificial intel-

The narrow ego-based identity and fears of the dominant section of humanity led to the treatment of nature and other species as hostile forces to be conquered triggering the ecological crisis that threatens human survival also.

ligence entity can become sentient and evolve into the cyber dimension of the Gaian web of life. The success of such endeavors depends on the integration of intuition into scientific and technological research. If scientific rationalism tries to integrate intuition as just another method without questioning the limitations of the scientific method itself, the result would cause more harm. The integration of intuition into scientific research in an effective way is possible only if the scientific establishment is forced to do a rethinking of the serious limitations and the anti-ecological, anti-intuitive, anti-feminine and even racist prejudices of the ideology of scientism and the scientific method itself. Such a rethinking could also help science to apply intuition and create technology that supports humanity's communion with Gaia.

Obstacles to Re-connecting with Earth

The obstacles to the restoration of the intuitive communion with Earth have both material and spiritual aspects. Both the excessive materialism of the Industrial Society pointed out by Cohen and the intensive Earth-weariness of many patriarchal religious and spiritual systems constitute a serious obstacle to the intuitive reconnection with Earth necessary for resolving the spiritual crisis of consciousness behind the physical ecological meltdown.

The disconnection from the life-giving intuitive connection to the spirit of the Earth can be traced back to an era that existed even before the advent of the Industrial Society that unleashed a mechanical worldview. When the Earth-oriented spirituality of ancient times was replaced by religious and spiritual systems that focused on patriarchal concepts, intuition and the understanding of Earth as a living presence were systematically suppressed. Organized religions that glorified a male creator God residing in a far away Heaven asserted the inferiority of Earth and their priesthood opposed any individual attempts to connect to the Divine through one's inner intuition. These patriarchal forces suppressed the knowledge and celebra-

tion of the Goddess (Walker, 2000). The patriarchal suppression of Goddess spirituality contributed to the alienation of human society from the Earth consciousness and intuition. Intuition was seen as a feminine faculty and discouraged. The patriarchal paradigm of command and control led to the glorification of the conquest of nature.

This resulted in the rise of fundamentalist religious ideologies that try to leave Earth behind. Even in the Eastern mystical spiritual traditions like the Mayavada teachings of the Indian Hindu monk Adi Sankara, there is a streak of illusionism, a dismissal of the material world and Earth as illusions. This is an idea, which only gained ground after its adherents actively suppressed the more integral Tantric traditions. The original pre-Vedic Tantric traditions of ancient India did not dismiss Earth and the manifested worlds as illusions though after the advent of patriarchy, even Tantric understanding became diluted with the introduction of the male God Shiva as a deity superior to the Goddess. Nowadays, most scholars of Tantra identify it with the Shiva-Shakti traditions (eg. Frost's 1999 book on Tantric Yoga). However, pre-Shaivite integral Tantric traditions did not see the Goddess as a secondary power of a male

primary God, and also considered our planet and the Cosmos as equally real manifestations of an integral multidimensional Ultimate Reality.

Sri Aurobindo had clearly indicated the inadequacy of Sankara's illusionism (Varma, 1998). In modern times, some ascensionist versions of the New Age movement consider the Earth as a lower dimension and hope to escape into ethereal non-physical dimensions, never to return (Maitreya, n.d.). Though these otherworldly versions of mystical traditions and New Age sects use some form of intuition in their practices, it is only an incomplete version of intuition that is far from integral, which explains their urge to separate from the Earth and physical dimensions. The followers of such dogma further distance themselves from the intuitive connection with Earth. To resolve the worsening ecological crisis, such outdated and exclusivist attitudes should be replaced with more inclusive and integral approaches that revitalize humanity's communion with Gaia.

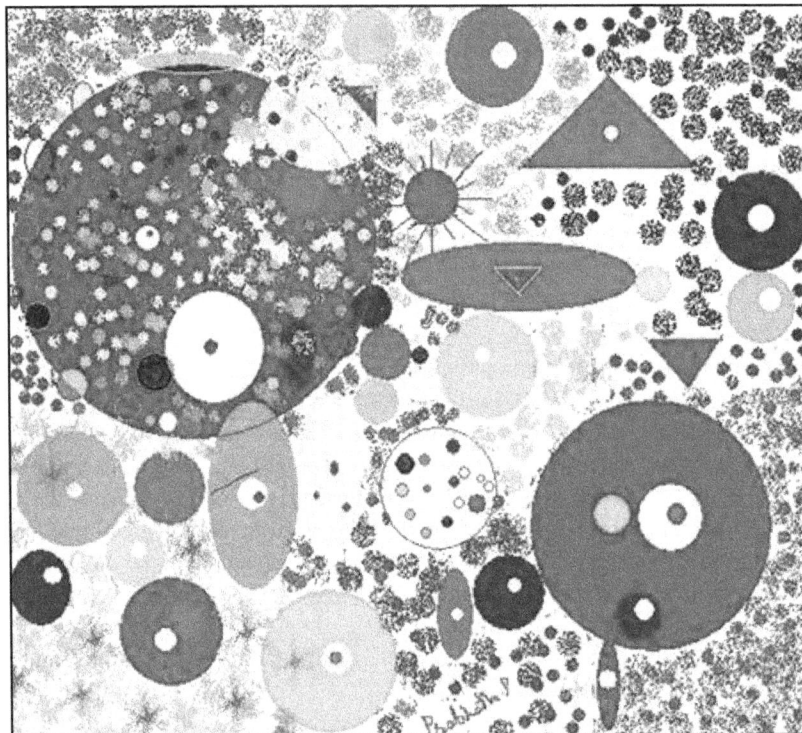

Communion — Image: Prabhath P ©2006

An Integral Gaia Yoga meditation for Communion with Gaia

I am presenting a glimpse of the meditative process for an integral intuitive communion with Gaia, from Integral Gaia Yoga (IGY), which I am developing based on long study, meditative practice and the inspiring example of my great-grandmother who was connected with an ancient and potent spiritual tradition that has been previously undocumented. A comprehensive introduction to Integral Gaia Yoga will be presented in the book I am working on. What is offered here is an inkling of Integral Gaia Yoga.

Integral Dimensions Meditation, a core aspect of Integral Gaia Yoga, uses breathing awareness for anchoring. The aim of this meditation is to intuitively experience many dimensions of reality in an integral way without ignoring any aspect. The following meditative exercise is intended to induce an integral intuitive communion with Gaia consciousness.

Choose a place for meditation amidst nature with minimum human interference. To experience the maximum effect, it is best to practice this meditation in a natural setting away from the cities plagued by pollution or mechanical noise. The most suitable time for this meditation is between 7 am and 8 am when the morning sunlight is warm, but not yet hot. Sit on the ground in a comfortable position. No yoga postures are necessary. What is important is that the sitting posture you use should not cause any physical discomfort to you. You can even sit on a chair with a backrest. Keep your spine straight and place the hands on your lap with the palms upward. Keep a glass of water, preferably taken from a natural source like a river, stream or lake, ready near you. Look at the natural scenery around you. Notice the greenery of trees and shrubs and the color of the soil. Look at any birds, insects or animals you see. Keep observing the natural surroundings for some time.

Now close your eyes. Touch the tips of the index finger with the tip of the thumb and keep the other three fingers straight, but relaxed. This is the sacred hand gesture called Gyan Mudra. Let the tip of your tongue touch the area where the inside of your upper gums and the upper teeth meet. Holding these hand and tongue positions in a relaxed manner during the meditation will help you to remain in a meditative awareness. These tongue and hand positions should be kept throughout the meditation.

Now pay attention to the flow of breathing at the tip of your nose without controlling the flow. Simply ride the

waves of inhalation and exhalation. You will find that your stomach goes out while you breathe in, and goes in while you breathe out. This is the natural way of breathing, which happens automatically when you are relaxed. There is no forced concentration, but only a relaxed attentive awareness.

Thoughts, the gaps of silence between thoughts, feelings, and body sensations are observed. No attempt is made to

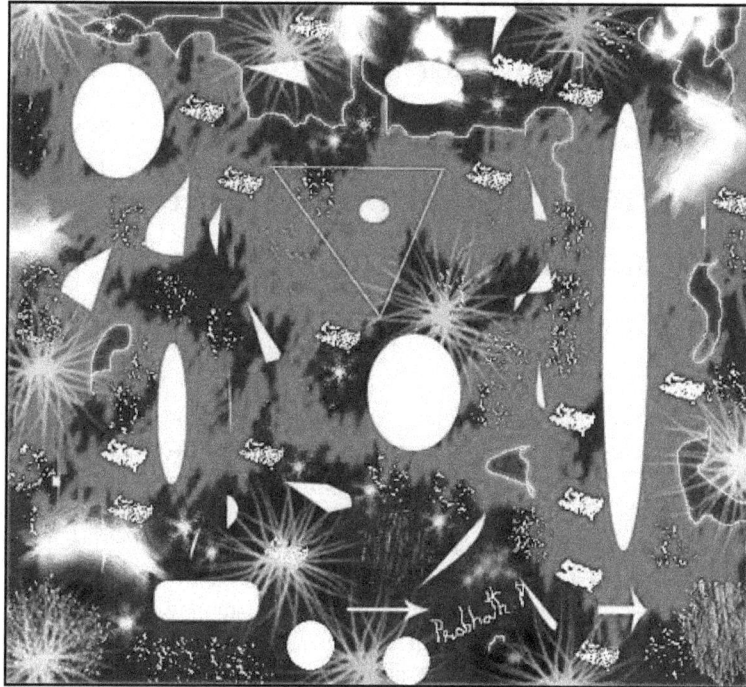

Order From Chaos — Image: Prabhath P ©2006

suppress these stimuli. Whatever you experience is witnessed in an unconditional and non-judgmental mindfulness without struggle or resistance. This puts you in a state of consciousness conducive to experience reality integrally and intuitively. Breathing awareness is used as the anchor to come back to, if your attention wanders too much from the meditative experience.

Visualize a Golden Flame in your heart centre. Imagine that it is your true soul, your authentic Self, an aspect of the Divine. Feel the comfortable warmth of the Golden Flame. Imagine the same Golden Flame burning in the heart of the Earth. You can also visualize the image of the Earth from outer space and see the Golden Flame in it. Feel the Golden Flame in you connecting with the Golden Flame of the Earth. Visualize yourself immersed within Gaia's Golden

Flame, which in turn is encompassed by the Golden Flame of the whole Cosmos against the background of a vast Transcendental Emptiness.

Now focus your attention more on the stimuli from nature, while keeping the eyes closed. Listen to the chirping of birds, sounds of any insects or animals and the wind rustling the leaves. Feel the sensation of the breeze brushing across your skin. Experience the warmth of the sunlight. All these sensations are part of the interactive conversation of the living Earth, Gaia, with you. If you hear the sound of a bird, imagine the Golden Flame in you connecting to the Golden Flame in the bird. Visualize you and the bird as parts of the Golden Flame of the Spirit of the Earth that spreads out from the core and envelops the whole planet. Realize that the air that you are breathing circulates through the whole biosphere of Gaia. Imagine you and all beings immersed within the protective envelope of Gaia's atmosphere. Do not try to verbalize what you experience. Just remain in communion with nature caressing you through this experience. Realize that you are not separate from Gaia. You are an integral part of Gaia's biosphere and consciousness. In that sense, your communion with Gaia is like being that communion itself.

Now gently open your eyes and again observe the visual richness of nature around you just as you did before the meditation. Wash your hands with water from the glass. Feel how the cool sensation of water differs from the warmth of the sunlight. Remind yourself that these different sensations are complementary aspects of the multidimensional "unity in diversity" of nature. Sit watching the natural area that surrounds you for a few more minutes and then slowly stand up concluding the meditation. But keep this experience of the aliveness of Gaia remain within you as you carry on with your daily life. This meditation, if practiced often, will help the meditators to experience Earth as a living organism rather than as an objectified environment that exists separate from humanity.

The Emerging Worldview

A worldview that values our intuitive connection with the web of life has been rising for some time despite the stiff resistance offered by the outdated dominant paradigm that thrives on the mindless plunder of the planet:

> The worldview now emerging - if we are bold to experience its implications - lets us behold anew and experience afresh the web of life in which we exist. It opens us to the vast intelligence of life's self-organizing powers, which have brought us forth from interstellar gases and primordial seas. It brings us to a larger identity in which to cradle and transcend our ego-identified fears. It lets us honor our pain for the world as a gateway into deep participation in the world's self-healing. (Macy & Brown, 1998, p.38)

My interpretation of the above comment of deep ecologist Joanna Macy and Brown is that the narrow ego-based identity and fears of the dominant section of humanity led to the treatment of nature and other species as hostile forces to be conquered triggering the ecological crisis that threatens human survival also. As the deep ecology movement exhorts, humanity should recognize the rights of all other species to blossom and flourish on Earth (Drengson & Inoue, 1995). Each strand in the web of life is important for the balance of the whole. The emerging worldview may be able to heal this rift and resolve the ecological imbalances by re-integrating humanity as a co-creative participant within the vast self-organizing network of Gaia consciousness.

It is undesirable to invest more energy into the mechanistic perspectives that separate mind and soul from matter or incomplete mystical approaches that utilize intuition only in partial ways as a means for a few chosen ones to escape into heavenly realms leaving Earth behind. The very survival and future evolution of humanity, other species and the Earth itself depend on the strengthening of an integral and intuitive worldview that values the well-being of the web of life. If humanity fails to adopt lifestyles that respect the integrity of the web of life, it is possible that the immune system of Gaian planetary organism may treat the human species as a disease-causing agent resulting in our extinction. The action we need to take includes a willingness to go beyond exclusive paradigms that separate us from Gaia and the creation of inclusive and ever-evolving approaches that strengthen humanity's communion with Gaia. So more than ever before, humanity and the planet now require an unprecedented acceptance of our integral intuitive and spiritual powers to enable cooperation, co-creation and communion with the life-enhancing consciousness of Gaia.

What needs to be questioned is not the existence of technology itself, but those technological applications, which follow the Industrial Society's mechanical model that harm the ecology and disrupt the human communion with Gaia.

References

Abram, D. (1984). The perceptual implications of Gaia. Reprint retrieved June 4, 2009, from http://www.bibliotecapleyades.net/gaia/esp_gaia10.htm

Auerbach, L. (1999). *Psychic Dreaming: A parapsychologist's handbook*. New York: Barnes & Noble.

Aurobindo, S. (1997). *Life divine* (12th ed.). Pondicherry, India: Aurobindo Ashram Publication Department. (Original work published 1939-40)

Capra, F. (1996). *The web of life: A new synthesis of mind and matter*. London: HarperCollins Publishers.

Cohen, M. J. (2008a). The green spirit of ecology and psychology: Educating, counseling and healing with nature through 53 naturals senses. Retrieved June 4, 2009 from http://www.ecopsych.com/kechnholspirit.html

Cohen, M. J. (2008b). *Educating, counseling and healing with nature: The science of natural attraction ecology: How to create moments that let Earth teach* (Electronic Version). Friday Harbor, Washington: Project NatureConnect, Institute of Global Education. Retrieved June 4, 2009, from http://www.ecopsych.com/ksanity.html

Day, L. (1996). *Practical intuition: How to harness the power of your instinct and make it work for you*. New York: Villard Books.

Drengson, A., & Inoue, Y. (Eds.). (1995). *The deep ecology movement: An introductory anthology*. Berkeley, California: Atlantic Books.

Ferrer, J., & Sherman, J. (Eds.). (2008). *The participatory turn: Spirituality, mysticism, religious studies*. Albany, NY: SUNY Press.

Frost G. (1999). *Tantric yoga: The royal path to raising Kundalini power*. (Y. Frost, Trans.). New Delhi: Motilal Banarsidass Publishers.

Gore, A. (2007). *The assault on reason*. New York: The Penguin Press.

Hanh, T. N., & Neumann, R. (2006). *Understanding our mind*. Berkeley, CA: Parallax Press.

Houghton, J. T. (2004). *Global warming: The complete briefing* (3rd ed.). Cambridge, UK: Cambridge University Press.

Lovelock, J. E. (1979). *Gaia: A new look at life on Earth*. Oxford, UK: Oxford University Press.

Macy, J., & Brown, M.Y. (1998). *Coming back to life: Practices to reconnect our lives, our world*. Gabriola Island, BC, Canada: New Society Publishers.

Maitreya (n.d.). Maitreya's teachings: Ascension. Retrieved May 25, 2009, from the Maitreya Educational Foundation Web site: http://www.maitreya-edu.org/teachings/ascnson.php

Satprem. (1996). *Sri Aurobindo or the adventure of consciousness* (3rd ed.). Paris: Institut de Recherches Evolutives. (Original work published 1970)

Varma, V.P. (1998). *The political philosophy of Sri Aurobindo*. New Delhi: Motilal Banarsidass Publishers.

Walker, B.G. (2000). *Restoring the Goddess: Equal rites for modern women*. Amherst, New York: Prometheus Books.

Waya, A.G. (n.d.). Chakras & vortexes of Mother Earth. Retrieved June 4, 2009 from http://www.innerself.com/Environmental/chakras.htm

Clairparlance
Activating Intuitive Communication

Matthew C. Bronson

A version of this article was originally co-authored with Dan Moonhawk Alford, my late colleague (1946-2002). Moonhawk's seminal thinking at the intersection of consciousness studies, linguistics and indigenous science can be accessed at http://www.enformy.com/alford.htm. "I," "we," and "our" refer to our joint experiences as linguistics instructors at the California Institute of Integral Studies (http://www.ciis.edu) during the 1980s and 1990s.

Not Just Words

A student of ours at the California Institute of Integral Studies reported in her journal that, while reading a favorite spiritual master, she entered into a state of mind characterized by "clear thinking, a clarity of perception entrained into an experience more aligned with a transformed perspective." She writes, "As I read, I could feel a change taking place in the mind. The content, which I don't recall, had nothing to do with it. But I began to grasp sections of the work as a whole, rather than word by word. And suddenly, my next step in life threw itself into relief; I saw exactly the

next and really only thing I could do - and proceeded to do it."

What is it that makes some communication in writing or in speech particularly impactful, even life-changing? How is it that a single book, conversation or speech can change your life while most everyday talk makes absolutely no discernible difference in the trajectory of your personal growth? Everyone has sat through a dull lecture, tried to read a boring book or listened to a friend talk

for two hours about their recent snorkeling trip to Ibiza while staring wistfully out the window and pretending to be interested. Most communication simply doesn't matter much in the scheme of things; it's about negotiating the scripts of life with minimal effort, playing the expected role of mother, son, boss, student, clerk, fan, heckler, and lubricating the machine of social life.

An alternate mode of communication is also available to all of us, one that will be the subject of this article. Sometimes, communication con-

nects heart and mind authentically in a way that breaks the habitual (but very fragile) thought-bubbles that separate rationality and intuition, one's soulful nature and the deeper aspects of Self so easily occluded in the samsara of everyday life. Think for a moment of communication that has really made a difference in your personal or spiritual development (a sermon, prayer, speech, poem, audience with a spiritual master, conversation with a counselor, pastor,

We cannot solve our problems with the same thinking we used when we created them.
Albert Einstein

teacher or intimate). What was going on? What was the quality of consciousness that you and others brought to the setting? What was the quality of the performance that supported or activated your experience?

Clairparlance is our word for the powerful communication form that directly inspires listeners or readers to transcend in some way their habitual internal dialogue and personal ego-boundaries. We distinguish this particular psi ability from clairvoyance, clairaudience, and clairsentience - psi powers traditionally

Matthew C. Bronson, Ph. D., see the above article *Lost and Found* for biographical information.

characterized by receptivity - because of the active quality of verbal communication. Yet while a clairparlant event originates with a speaker's active projection of higher consciousness through language, the impact of his communication depends equally on the quality of the audience's listening or reading experience. A clairparlant event is thus not merely a function of words, but of the entire setting in which the act takes place and the evolving consciousness of the listener or reader.

Our task in this article is to inquire into the structure and process of clairparlance, in the aim of enhancing readers' personal and professional lives with a renewed appreciation for language as the interplay between being and doing. In this connection we quote Benjamin Whorf, the pioneering linguist and spiritual father of our study:

> We all know now that the forces studied by physics, chemistry, and biology are powerful and important. People do not generally know that the forces studied by linguistics are powerful and important, that its principles control every sort of agreement and understanding among humans, and that sooner or later it will have to sit as judge while the other sciences bring their results to its court to inquire into what they mean. (Whorf, 1956: 232)

People who have experienced a moving sermon, an inspiring book or lecture, or the healing words of a trance channel can attest to the uplifting effect of clairparlant acts; in rendering us transparent witnesses to the ongoing miracle of our natures, such communications make us co-creators of both personal and collective realities. The capacity for clear-speaking and clear-writing, however, is not reserved for our heroes of communication like Shakespeare, Socrates, and Mohandas Gandhi. These "warriors of the words" were simply embodiments of a capacity that is the birthright of all humanity.

Clairparlance as Personal Best

Although we will refer in our definition of clairparlance to the communications of renowned social activists and spiritual masters, it is important to remember that anyone can enter a clairparlant mode, and thereby create a clear-

ing for discovery in his thousand little acts of everyday speech and writing. As a step in our personal evolution, as an affirmation of our whole being, we can make literally every word count by observing and listening to not only our "great communicators," but to our colleagues and ourselves as well. After all, we live in almost constant communication by our very nature. "Man, considered as a species, is one of the singing kind, except his notes refer to ideas." W. Von Humboldt, creator of linguistics as a discipline, reminds us that the study of clairparlance can lead us to the finest, most powerful language-songs, while inviting us to join in with our own clear voice.

We have all had clairparlant moments at one time or another; we've been in the "clairparlant groove." Those who teach or speak publicly often have moments (like a colleague of ours recently reported) when the lecture flows spontaneously and elegantly from our lips in a way that completely fits the moment, without our having to search or grope for the exactly appropriate words. Our listeners sit wide-eyed on the edges of their seats, as if we were voicing for them some latent truth of their own experience. Some of us have comforted a friend with a healing dance of word and gesture. Others have transcended a seemingly insurmountable obstacle in a negotiation process by a single, joyful sleight of tongue. These moments are windows on our clairparlant nature through which language, as a living thing, intersects with our self, as living being. During such times, a highly charged, precise version of ordinary language courses through us, and we experience ourselves as conduits for the fundamental logos.

Some Characteristics of Clairparlance

This direct tapping into the underlying logos may not seem as novel to all peoples as it does to us in modern Western Culture. Clairparlance appears to be a practice more cultivated in tradi-

tionally oral cultures, such as that of the Native American. Indeed, some Native American oratory, even after translation into English, presents a standard of clairparlance challenged only by the greatest poets and orators of Western civilization.

A primary characteristic of clairparlance is the frequent use of sensory images to deliver the intended feeling tone as a direct experience for the listener. Using images of taste and smell, the Chief quickens our own primal urge to remember these senses, so often taken for granted:

> The white man does not seem to notice the air he breathes. Like a man dying for many days, he is numb to the stench. But if we sell you our land, you must remember that the air is precious to us, that the air shares its spirit with all the life it supports. The wind that gave our grandfather his first breath also receives his lost sigh. And the wind must also give our children the spirit of life. And if we sell you our land, you must keep it apart and sacred, as a place where even the white man can go to taste the wind that is sweetened by the meadow's flowers. [1]

Another characteristic of clairparlant texts is the rhythmic alternation between concrete (i.e., sensory) and abstract

What you are doing speaks so loudly, that I cannot hear what you say.
Ralph Waldo Emerson

images. This technique is particularly evident in the form of the power metaphor as a special class of metaphor that goes beyond the mere comparison of unlike things, to open a flood of new significance on an old idea. When Martin Luther King Jr. invited his people, in his famous speech to "bathe in the warm waters of mercy," he compressed the abstract concept of mercy into a forceful sensory experience; Winston Churchill galvanized the attitude of a generation with his use of the term "Iron Curtain" to symbolize the perceived communist domination of Eastern Europe; and for

---

[1] While the authenticity of this translated text and its fidelity to the Chief's words to white settlers in 1854 are in dispute, we present it here as an exemplar of sensorily rich language that is typical of Native American sacred speech. See http://www.chiefseattle.com/history/chiefseattle/speech/speech.htm for a full text of the speech and a discussion.

centuries Plato vividly characterized the debate over human duality with his image of man as a charioteer harnessing a black and a white horse, representing his Appolonian and Dionysian aspects.

Mind, so that it has the capacity to draw you into that Disposition, that Company, that Radiance, that Realization.[2]

The idea that mantric speech can directly transform the listener has been

LaViolette feeling tone model of cognition (LaViolette, 1986), which holds that all thoughts are special emotional sequences. Reasoning from this model, it would follow that to achieve clairparlance in our own lives we must first contact the specific feeling tones we wish to share in a communication. The appropriate words, phrases, and intonation would then be attracted to these tones as iron filings to a magnet, or as birds to the shoulder of St. Francis. (See Bronson, 2004 for application of this idea to public speaking).

How is it that a single book, conversation or speech can change your life while most everyday talk makes absolutely no discernible difference in the trajectory of your personal growth?

In these and many more instances, a superbly apt blending of the sensory with the abstract imbues expression with a lasting and compelling grace.

Feeling Tones and Clairparlant Masters

The language of spiritual masters and visionaries is often memorable for its underlying feeling tones or emotional style. The letters and speeches of Mohandas Gandhi, which moved millions to action and changed the course of modern history, were powered by the engine of his unflagging passion: "Life to me would lose all interest if I felt that I could not attain perfect love on earth," he wrote to his son. "After all, what matters is that our capacity for loving ever expands" (Erickson, 1969, p. 316). The transforming and healing powers of the words of Gandhi, and of the many others whom we recognize as harbingers of eternal truths, are owed in large part to the forceful field of universal love from which their communication springs.

Recall the opening story about the student who had a clairparlant experience while reading. Especially notable in this account is the relative insignificance of content in the message's impact. The master she was reading explained his special kind of language as mantric speech:

My teaching is a form of ecstatic speech, and ecstatic speech is mantric. My speech and writings are not composed of 'oms' and 'hrirs' and similar mantras, but they are nevertheless mantric. The Teaching is a direct reflection of the Transcendental

the province of sages and shamans throughout the eons, and its connection with clairparlance is worth exploring.

Mantra, which is a form of language in its non-referential aspect, is said to bring about a settling, healing state through a general relaxation of the "muscles of the mind." (Yogi, 1963). Participation in a clairparlant event introduces a similar state in which individuals report profound emotional and physiological effects that are more lasting and meaningful than the specific content of the communication. Clairparlance washes over the audience like a wave of feeling-charged mantra cleansing the mind-body, as does deep meditation, leaving in its wake a memory of sequential emo-

Such a model also would explain why obsessive preoccupation with the surface level of language, with finding the right words, often disrupts a communicator's fluency, and why words spoken in the "clairparlant groove" seem to flow in a steady, even stream, ready for use as they are needed. This is surely how it was for the prophets of the Old Testament; according to tradition, their speech was channeled directly from the divine nature without critical reflection. "To everything there is a season, and a time for every purpose under heaven" (Ecclesiastes). In the time for speaking or writing, clairparlance, that inspiring enrapturing, may be invited by the intellect but not directed by it. Clairparlance is ever in the season of the heart.

Trance Channeling and Clairparlance

The calling to channel is neither vague

For the shaman, it is as if existence were uttering itself through him ... words are materializations of consciousness; language is a privileged vehicle of our relation to reality.

tional tones, and a sense of the personal changes induced.

Corresponding to the concept of feeling tones as the fundamental organizing principle of consciousness is the Gray-

[2] Da Free John (Franklin Jones) cited in a student journal. Original reference unavailable. For similar teachings from this same teacher and period see (Jones, 1973).

nor easily ignored (Bronson, 1985, 1992). Typical of the personal accounts of initiation into channeling is that of the Ibn Arabi (1165-1240), who viewed his writings as "a way out of the fire of inspiration" — fire which he sometimes feared might burn him up. By his own account, William Blake's words were born of his conversations with angels and the divine burning within his soul. His "Tyger, tyger burning bright / in the forests of the night," is a potent symbol of the vibrant force that propelled him to create the poems and paintings for which he is famous.

Although the word clairparlance is new to our language, the knowledge of its power stretches far back into mythological and biblical texts. Speaking the intent of the Gods was commonplace in antiquity; the Delphic oracle and the angelic voices of Hildegard of Bingen and St. Teresa are but three examples.

An eloquent expression of 18th century thinking on the subject arose through the following words of Emanuel Swedenborg, a scientist and psi-technician who profoundly influenced Blake and many others:

> The words which Spirits utter, that is, which they excite or call forth out of a man's memory, and imagine to be their own, are well chosen and clear, full of meaning, distinctly pronounced, and applicable to the subject spoken of; and, what is surprising, they know how to choose expressions much better and more readily than the man himself; nay, as was shown above, they are acquainted with the various significations of words, which they apply instantaneously, without any premeditation; by reason, as just observed, that the ideas of their language flow only into those expressions which are best adapted to signify their meaning. The case, in this respect is like that of a man who speaks without thinking at all about his words, but is intent only on their sense; when his thought falls readily, and spontaneously, into the proper expressions. It is the sense inwardly intended that calls forth the words. In such inward sense, but of a still more subtle and excellent nature, consists the speech of spirits and by which man, although he is ignorant of it, has communication with them. (as cited in Schwartz, 1978, p. 278).

For the alchemists, mystics, and visionaries who are our historical antecedents, the intervention of spirit in channeling is no anomaly or miracle, but a necessary indication of the eternal unity of spirit, mind, and body. From their view, the "bizarre" facts of channeling needn't be squared with the rationalistic scheme that posits an abyss between spirit and body-mind.

Repetition

Repetition of words, drumbeats, mantra, and other repetitious sounds has been part of the technology of consciousness alteration since prehistory, and still shows up in the clairparlant discourses of master hypnotists and orators alike. Clairparlants normally also make special use of personal references: Martin Luther King, Jr.'s famous "I have a dream" repeated strategically in the adlibbed part of his speech gradually collapsed all the individual "I"s of the audience into an encompassing intersubjectivity that found its voice in his own.

Clairobics and Neurolinguistic Programming (NLP)

Clairparlance is a power - seen, felt, and heard - that can be harnessed in many ways as a healing technique to counter the common communicative

Clairparlance is ever in the season of the heart.

Clairparlance is our word for the powerful communication form that directly inspires listeners or readers to transcend in some way their habitual internal dialogue and personal ego-boundaries

impasses that confront us in both our personal and professional lives. Neurolinguistic Programming (NLP), a set of principles and techniques now enjoying much popularity, offers an elegant model for analysis of subjective human experience, including the clairparlant act, in terms of the senses. By making sensory distinctions among human behavior patterns, NLP can actually replicate many instances of exceptional human performance, particularly in communication. Thus, the essence of clairparlance is to

first establish rapport, an empathic bond between speaker and listener (see Bronson, 1996 for a practical example of how to do this).

A deeper understanding of clairparlance can also be used to stretch our communicative essence, as we do our bodies, in the form of "clairobics." Writer's block is a common manifestation of difficulty in communication. Clairparlance teaches us that attention to the flow of emotional tones behind, beneath, or around the flow of communication can reveal the roots of our inability to get on with the writing process. "What are the specific emotional tones of my intent and what is their appropriate sequence in my message?" is a more empowering self-inquiry for the writer than "What are the right words for me to say?" Movement, art, music, meditation can all serve as exploratory modes in preparation for important communication in writing or speech. As the feelings flow, so flow the words.

The fear of public speaking is one pervasive form of speaker's block, where once again, the lessons of clairparlance can be applied (Bronson, 2004). A first principle of clairparlance is the necessity of getting free from self-consciousness, which frequently obstructs our own true voice. This can be as simple as two or three minutes of deep diaphragmatic breathing. (It is physiologically impossible to be anxious and breathing from the diaphragm at the same time!) By studying and witnessing clairparlance at every opportunity, we can absorb the strategies of confidence and power and make them our own, while transcending the limitations of our native skills. We can discover our own clairparlant natures in this process and thus become more powerful speakers and writers in our own right.

Specific instruction in communication skills derived from studies like clairobics and NLP could be profitably included in the curriculum of preparation for many professions. Teachers in particular could benefit from training in facilitation of discussion, rapport-building and the delivery of captivating lecture, using an enhanced repertoire of communicative strategies. Managers, sales people, and medical practitioners of all stripes also could benefit profoundly from a heightened grasp of the power of the word. Clairparlance is a power to heal, to move, to bring out thoughts and feelings into a physical form. It is a power at home with our humanity.

The Path of Clairparlance

This paper is offered as but one chapter in the ongoing revelation of the principles of clairparlance. Asian cultures have long recognized that the study of the phenomenon can lead to better access to spiritual truths. In the Hindu tradition, clairparlance is seated in the fifth chakra, which, when awakened and opened (especially in conjunction with the heart and third-eye chakras) calls forth clear-speaking of the truth. The Buddha advocates "Right Speech" as a facet of the Eightfold Path, emphasizing its centrality to the process of enlightenment:

> One naturally has to speak the truth, has to use words that are friendly and benevolent, pleasant and gentle, meaningful and useful. One should not speak carelessly; speech should be at the right time and place. If one cannot say something useful, one should keep noble silence. (Rahula, 1974, p. 47)

In the West, the recent revival of interest in the psychotherapeutic significance of language has placed special emphasis on such "verbal hygiene" in the healing process (Boorstein, 1985).

The modern therapist, however, tends to heal by listening. Perhaps it is time to re-valorize in parallel the ancient technologies of shamanism inherited from Paleolithic times, with their focus on healing through speech. In the following description of the language of the shaman under the influence of the sacred mushroom, we find a compelling summary of the power of clairparlance:

> The Mazatecs say that the mushrooms speak. At times it is as if one were being told what to say, for the words leap to mind, one after another, of themselves, without having to be searched for: a phenomenon similar to the automatic dictation of the surrealists, except that here the flow of consciousness, rather than being disconnected, tends to be coherent: a rational enunciation of meanings. Message fields of communication with the world, others, and oneself are disclosed by the mushroom. The spontaneity they liberate is not only perceptual, but linguistic, the spontaneity of speech, of fervent, lucid discourse, of the logos in activity. For the shaman, it is as if existence were uttering itself through him ... words are materializations of consciousness; language is a privileged vehicle of our relation to reality (Munn, 1973, pp.88-89).

It has been precisely the intent here to present "language as a privileged vehicle of our relation to reality." This has been written with the goal of inspiring you to bring an enhanced quality of mindfulness to your speech and writing, for with your words you create your reality in some large measure. As students of clairparlance, we can more mindfully infuse our humanity into the worlds we are co-creating with each breath and word.

References

Boorstein, S. (1985). Notes on right speech as a psychotherapeutic technique. *Journal of Transpersonal Psychology, 17*(1), 47-56.

Bronson, M. C. (2004). Harnessing the butterflies: A new approach to public and private speaking, *ReVision, 26*(4), 33-36.

Bronson, M. C. (1996). Pace and lead: The grammar of rapport. *The Anthropology of Consciousness, 7*(1), 34-38.

Bronson, M. C. (1992). When as-if becomes as-is: The spontaneous initiation of a Brazilian spiritist medium. *The Anthropology of Consciousness, 3*(1-2), 45-62.

Bronson, M. C. (1985). Brazilian spiritist healers, *Shaman's Drum*, Winter Issue, 23-28. Retrieved June 19, 2009 from http://www.enformy.com/dma-braz.htm

Erickson, E. M. (1969). *Gandhi's truth*. New York: M. Morton & Co.

Jones, F. (1973). *The method of the Siddhas*. Los Angeles: Dawn Horse Press.

LaViolette, P. (1986). Teaching with feeling in mind. *On the Beam, 6*(2), 10-15.

Yogi, M. M. (1963). *Transcendental meditation*. New York: New American Library.

Munn, H., (1973). The mushrooms of language. In Michael Harner (Ed.), *Hallucinogens and shamanism* (pp. 86-122). New York: Oxford University Press.

Rahula, W. (1959). *What the Buddha taught*. New York: Grove Press.

Schwartz, L. (1975). *The occult and the supernatural*. New York: Crown Publishers.

Whorf, B. (1956). *Language, thought and reality*. Cambridge: M.I.T. Press.

Children's Texts Facilitated by J. Ruth Gendler:

People Said the World Will Change in Time

Riley Felt (At Age 9)

Creativity exploded into the world. Beings stared in awe as it shot across the sky, with words, music, and color falling from the clouds.

She was born from Laughter and Fierce. Laughter giggled at her daughter and Creativity smiled and cooed back. Fierce expanded and gave Creativity will to push on. Thus, Creativity boomed.

When she softly fell to Earth, she gave the world color. People and animals alike jumped with Joy by their side. Creativity infected the sky, which rained down the same will Fierce gave Creativity. People all over jumped to grab their share from the air. Afterwards, Creativity stretched across the sky, making a rainbow. Later on, Joy and Creativity became inseparable, and hid behind corners, waiting to consume an unexpected someone.

People said the world will change in time.
Little did they know the world has already changed
and still was. Even though they thought, "Everything is same,"
Birds will fly, people will laugh, creatures will grow, wind
will blow. But – the wind is blowing. The creatures are
growing. The people are laughing. And the little birds
are flying.
"Run with me!" Cried the sun, chasing time across the sky.
"Shine with me!" Shouted the moon, trying to out-bright time.
"Dance with us!" Chorused the stars, tangoing time.
"Stay still with me," Whispered time, "And ride upon my
blowing, create upon my growing, peoplize with my laughs, and
see within my flying." "No" Complained the beings. "We
want to run, and shine, and dance!"
Time laughed. "Look around you. You already are."
But humans, creatures, winds, and birds never noticed. They were
with time, attached with time, no matter what.
And time laughed.

Heart Mountain by Ruth Gendler, acrylic on paper

A Trip Down the Milkman's Way
(written to Ruth Gendler's painting *Heart Mountain*)

If you walk down the Milkman's Way, on a star-spangled night,
and take a stroll past Saturn's Ringstore, you'll find the
spoon that ran away with the fork in the road.
Turn round wise, and continue until you see a hole
in the sky. Or rather, a window. There is no key, no door,
no glass, and no sound pours out, only rose petals spattered
with purple, orange, and pale. The only black in this hole
is a cat who jumped over the sun. His name is
Nacho. It matches the warm feeling of his heart, and
spice of his nature. Don't judge this cat by his fur.
The black hair opens up to a rainbow of mind.
Who owns this cat? No, not who, but what. If you take a peek through
this window, the explosion of color comes from an orange
volcano. The what who opened up your mind.
Don't be afraid. Slide into the hole. Go on,
See what's behind the Mirror of Mind.

J. Ruth Gendler is the author of *Notes on the Need for Beauty, Changing Light: The Eternal Cycle of Night & Day*, and *The Book of Qualities*. She teaches creative writing to children and adults. All examples in this issues are from her classes. On the web she can be found at www. redroom.com/author/j-ruth-gendler.

The Ecology of Intuition

From Crisis to Opportunity

Arupa L. Tesolin

As we find ourselves in the midst of a global restructuring that is causing massive change in economies, business and trade, jobs and lifestyles, what impact can intuition have on the inevitable rebalancing of both our ledgers and economic and societal values? What influence does intuition have on our world, individuals, businesses and organizations? What would happen if we started looking more deeply at the importance of intuition? What if people were able to understand its causal linkages with economics, lifestyle, business, education, health and the environment? If the value of intuition were to increase, how would the world change? Would a greater concentration on developing intuition capabilities, and consequently a new neural footprint, improve our future? What new questions are worthy of exploration and dialogue? To emerge from a world in crisis, intuition may play a crucial role.

The ecology of intuition is a topic

Arupa L. Tesolin is a speaker, trainer, consultant and global thought leader on intuition, innovation and creative capital. She is the author of *Ting!: A surprising way to listen to intuition & do business better*, and *Spark: Raise your mind to the power of infinity & create anything*. Arupa owns the corporate training company Intuita and her Web site is www.intuita.com.

that, in the light of our formidable crises and challenges, can help us strip down and re-think what it means to be human in a modern world. The world, as we have grown it to date, has become one that is ideally suited to "human-havings" and "human-doings," mostly in tandem, since one necessitates the other. It seems less well adapted to foster "human-beings." The quest for material satisfaction has often outpaced and displaced other human needs. My hope is that wiser minds can and should prevail in helping to lead the next quadrant of our human unfolding.

Intuition has many points of impact. Its underlying linkages and their connections, when understood in the proper context, affect the greater proportion of our lives and institutions. The value of intuition exerts a direct and potentially measurable impact on learning, business, science, health, environment, human relations and conflict resolution. Each of the areas mentioned above influence and impact individuals, economies and societies. When the value of intuition changes, even minimally, at a personal level, it acts as a lever to trigger much larger change at systemic levels.

This paper is set out as the beginning of a discussion on these connected topics. My hope is that others will contribute to these ideas and assist in developing them. Other, obvious preliminary questions include: What is the role of intuition in our lives and on society?

Why is intuition important?

In answering these questions we must also ask how increasing the importance of intuition can shape individual, community, business, environmental and societal values? And what can people and organizations do individually and collectively to effectively develop intuition? Then, if we can accomplish this, how would it benefit us and society?

Most dictionaries define intuition as knowing without thinking but do not state what the significance of intuition is. Most people studying intuition get bogged down in it as a highly individual sensory experience, also called phenomenology, rather than the wisdom it imparts. All accounts suggest, particularly ancient Vedic texts, that intuitive intelligence precedes the senses. Intuitive thought is regarded as pure thought while thoughts processed and interpreted via the senses are regarded as impure thought (Sen 2005). We have learned to rely on our sensory experience, not our being. Investigating sensory intuitive experience might waste time, but developing increased intuitive awareness could yield great benefits.

Currently we use intuition as an intellectual default mechanism. When facts aren't enough, intuition incorporates our creative energy to extend our knowledge and solve problems. Intuition's value rises the most during changing times or when precedents are absent and when creative solutions are required to understand and solve complex issues and problems. The current period of rapid and discontinuous change provides a very fertile ground for the use of increased intuition.

Intuition, Self and Human Engineering

Intuition, in its purest form, is the basic knowledge of the universe, which supplants our intellectual processes. Most of us remain patently under-skilled in intuitive know-how. Western education processes, dominant in global education, typically displace this knowledge by favoring analytical and comparative reasoning. Religious institutions reveal enough knowledge to keep the faithfulness of their community intact. Traditional spiritual and alternative lifestyle communities lean toward a limited view of a world based on their often utopian notions, a world that would bore the pants off most people now inhabiting an increasingly urban planet.

By contrast, various schools of yoga and meditative practice have become quite successful in developing advanced intuition for their followers, who often live wonderful and fulfilling lives while contributing actively to their families, communities, business and society. This is a very powerful and empowering outcome and one worthy of further exploration.

Intuition has had both proponents and detractors. Typically, only a small proportion of people in any population experience heightened intuitive sensitivity. Because of this, the personal experience of intuition has been regarded as an exceptional skill of people such as psychics and others, including saints and gurus, whose seemingly superconscious abilities were seen as anomalies. Often these discussions centered around proving or disproving the existence of intuition, or crediting or discrediting intuitive experience rather than developing it.

While the extreme abilities were often confined to gurus and saints, they often taught specialized techniques to their population of followers who experienced expanded spiritual and intuitive awareness. Development of intuition was self-evident at an individual level. Beyond this, a circle of either believers or non-believers, depending on which camp they were in, would consort. Comparably, believers who followed some sort of development practice saw direct results while non-believers either looked for a plausible explanation according to their beliefs or sought reasons to discredit or disprove the experience of the others. This has led to the polarization of believers and non-believers rather than to building common understanding and collective development of intuition.

Western education approaches, continue to favor developing the intellect, comparative analyses and critical thinking skills. Intuition is still vastly under-rated as a skill. While intelligent comparative analysis is important, computers are now often better at processing volumes of data than humans. Achieving this productivity milestone raises the question, "What is the true purpose of the human mind?" Intuitively, this question suggests that humans were designed to create and to conceive beyond the intellectual mind. Scientists have charted so far only a small portion of our capabilities. Therefore, a vast proportion of human abilities still exist beyond science. Anecdotally, we realize that the results created by developing and experimenting with intuitive and creative abilities will likely out-pace the speed at which science will be able to explain, prove and quantify them.

By increasing the importance and scope of intuition in consciousness science, currently the least researched sub-topic in this field, more research funding can be directed to studying intuition mechanics and development so that we can better understand and evaluate its impact on our perceptions, decisions and ultimately the fulfillment of our lives. To be more purposeful and fruitful, research needs to shift away from validating personal intuition experience, made scientifically difficult by the need to quantify first person experience toward identifying linkages and applications.

Some consciousness researchers are still searching for the neural correlates of consciousness, or rather the place where the wires of consciousness map onto the human body. With intuition they may find these roots exposed in the self-limiting subjectivity of conventional science, which is more like a two-dimensional rabbit hole on paper than the fourth dimensional world it represents. Scientists themselves are the subjective arbiters of their own world. As they change, their world emerges more fully into the real.

The question of consciousness is perhaps the most significant problem still unsolved by science. It is no wonder that the problem of consciousness has been regarded as perhaps the most significant question that still remains unsolved by science. Consciousness is literally a matter of life and death; you exist only insofar as your subjective reality exists. (Revonsuo, 2009, Prologue p.16)

More research funding should be committed to studying the role and relationship of intuition and sense perception with a view to understanding how the mechanics of intuition and its intricate relationship with our nerves, senses and self-chemistry can make a difference in our lives. We need to study differ-

Intuition's value rises the most during changing times or when precedents are absent and when creative solutions are required to understand and solve complex issues and problems.

ent ways to develop intuition and what impact each of these have on perception, learning, happiness, decision-making, stress, creativity and innovation.

At a personal level, most people can identify with the experience of receiving intuition about an important pending situation and choosing to ignore it, often to their own detriment. The reasons they ignore their intuition vary by individual and by situation. These reasons range from a lack of experience or confidence in trusting their intuition and personal preferences, sensory processing habits and resistance to change. Even wishful thinking can have the effect of suppressing intuition. This is what happens when a person keeps on hoping for a different outcome, rather than choosing to respond to the intuitive information he or she has received. Learning more about the psychology of intuition response would be beneficial to anyone's understanding about why we sometimes choose to ignore intuition's important signals. Such learning could open the door to greater and more conscious functionality of our own beingness.

The potential benefits of greater personal intuition skills can't be underestimated. The quality of our intuitive experience influences every decision we take in our lives – from choosing a potential mate to experiencing, creating and communicating in every relationship, our physical and mental well-being, investments, job, career and business choices, artistic pursuits, hobbies, the ability to accurately assess opportunities, maintain family connections, personal perceptions, time management, stress, authenticity, clarity, happiness and a sense of spiritual union or connection with the universe.

By making the benefits of a higher personal intuition experience more explicit among the general population and increasing the availability and accessibility after training and information, humanity stands to advance considerably at both a personal and collective level.

Defining an optimal level of intuition function at this point would have merit in influencing the attainment of high intuition function as a desirable state. Perhaps an optimal level would go something like this: A high-functioning person on the intuitive scale would

be someone who has attained a somewhat defined level of intuition mastery, with a balance in both intuition and reasoned intelligence, who both wisely directs and is directed by a keen sense of intuitive knowledge and purpose, whose self-interest and compassionate public interest is generally unified, while

Intuition, in its purest form, is the basic knowledge of the universe, which supplants our intellectual processes. Most of us remain patently under-skilled in intuitive know-how.

being aware generally of the opinions and developing conditions around him/her. From there we can identify levels of intuition functionality that are on a lesser scale of functioning and define other levels that may signify a level of intuitive impairment.

Intuition and Learning

It takes surprisingly little effort to train ourselves to be more intuitive, probably much less than has been needed to educate ourselves to become functionally analytical. The basics of training typically amount to some combination of self-reflective practice, meditation techniques, and application.

The connection between intuition and learning are fascinating and generate interesting questions about how the two properties interact, link and enable each other. How does a higher intuition level promote faster or more effective learning? More research aligned with intuition and skills or talent development, intuitive and neural development, how intuition may assist in overcoming developmental and learning disabilities, and fostering more intuitive approaches to learning pedagogy should help us to answer these questions.

In some undetermined future time, we may all learn new skills by electronically or biomechanically applying an advanced neural intuitive program

to help create the synaptic pre-conditions that enable us to learn and master that skill faster. An increased value and role of intuition can potentially be very effective in the video-game and learning industry, and the fusion of learning, gaming, experiential, motor and cognitive skills development.

The personal intuitive development of the general public has exceeded academic research and study in intuition. It's worth mentioning that the anecdotal impact and development advice, offered by countless self-help books that feed and guide personal development trends and experiential learning, has contributed significantly to collective learning about intuition. Widespread electronic access to quality learning material has accelerated this trend.

There is good reason to now bring intuition practice into the fold of a well-balanced junior education system to prepare young people to manage their own internal resources. This way, they can benefit from having reduced stress, while achieving superior problem-solving capabilities and higher personal fulfillment. In India, yoga is taught as part of a general school curriculum to help calm and balance the mind. Other cultures would be wise to learn from India's experience and leadership in this regard.

Intuition is used to distinguish and distill the essence of good information from collective information muck, because we now have access to so much information that it has become a distraction. Instinctively we recognize the enormous power of having a connected world that can now distribute learning and awareness instantaneously, thereby having created the capability to immediately raise consciousness and know-how on any matter simultaneously. We have become one mind.

Intuition and the Science of Business

In February 2009, the Canadian Society of Management Accountants published an article I wrote on "Intuition as a Sustainable Business Advantage." In May 2009, the Ontario branch created a new Leadership award that recognizes the outstanding efforts of their members in intuition, attributed to generating successful ideas and solutions from a divergent thinking perspective – a.k.a. "thinking outside the box." This category is alongside others for imagination, innovation and big ideas.

climate change and determining the size and costs of our "carbon footprint." Only when cost accountants began to derive monetary values for the size of this footprint through new directions in accounting theory and practice, did the movers and shakers of the world begin to really pay attention and make new decisions. The bottom line is that when accountants pay attention, everything changes.

above once again, the model of "think outside the box" has shown up. So, how about this box? Where did it come from? And how do we see outside of it? We all say the words from time to time, "think outside the box." This appears to be current industry-speak for intuition. But last time I regarded the human brain, it looked like anything but a box. So, where did that box come from? The box is actually a mental model that started when the world changed to an industrialized society and began to devise ways to customize mass production of material goods and communicate how this was done. The box became the common model to illustrate how materials were broken down, processed and distributed. Gradually this model became incorporated by habit into our thinking process and then was extended into the conceptualization of most fields including information management.

Traditional spiritual and alternative lifestyle communities lean toward a limited view of a world based on their often utopian notions, a world that would bore the pants off most people now inhabiting an increasingly urban planet.

Most CMA members occupy the trusted status of a chief financial officer, executive manager or comptroller for public, institutional, government and private businesses. These are the people who manage the balance sheets, eliminate waste, evaluate assets, help determine strategic business plans and provide management advice to keep their corporations profitable. The existence of this award makes a profound statement to both members and Canadian executives and also to corporate executives around the world – that intuition can be connected with profit, innovation and leadership. Here is an association that is leading the way and thinking about tomorrow.

I was invited by one of the local chapters to attend Devamrita Swami's April 2009 lecture on "Spiritual Accounting" to CMA accountants. In it, the Yale-trained economist and monk spoke about the important role that accountants have in influencing what societies value. He said that accountants exert an important influence because they ascribe how things are valued and what matters. Accordingly, these assessments determine what society values by affecting both how markets respond and how people live their lives. A direct example of how accountants affect societal values includes assessing the global impact of

Contrast this with the 2009 state of the global automotive industry – now fanning the flames of the virtual hell the industry created for itself caused by its arrogant inability to persistently drive innovation value and respond to a changing consumer market. In January, I was called as an "out of the box" thinker to lead the Innovation Panel for the World Automotive News Congress. This is a collective of the global automotive industry held in Detroit, the birthplace of the world's mass production vehicle manufacturing plants and very close to the birthplace of a young visionary engineer named Henry Ford who in the 1900's started making the dream of every worker being able to own a car a reality. While I was there, I saw an industry in the throes of its own desperation. Meanwhile, the casualties of this industry persist amid many influence factors, which include the political predilections of the oil industry, which helped to influence this painful outcome.

You may have noticed in the example

With its obvious limitations as far as complex systems and human beings are concerned, the box has become too constrained as a model to contain our growing comprehension of implicit knowledge, our own beingness, and the complexity of the world around us. This model represents the epitome of linear reductionism, on which traditional science is based, which attempts to break everything down into its smallest components, in order to understand how it works. Reductionism has its limitations because complex systems and human beings aren't easily reduced to boxes or to atoms for that matter.

Intuition is the source for imagination because it represents knowledge that arises from the unknown.

The importance of intuition in innovation cannot be overstated. Intuition is the source for imagination because it represents knowledge that arises from the unknown, rather than from memory and prior experience. All innovation occurs as a result of identifying some new constituent or novel application or a twist on an old application applied in a different arena. Here, intuition appears to have a fundamental and vital role.

As the new dawn of the innovation age arises, every employee, manager, team and business owner needs to have a basic grasp of their intuition capabilities and ideally some training so that they are able to fruitfully grow, identify and seize opportunities for new product and service innovations. But in today's world anyone can be an innovator, from the 6th grade student to an artist, a stay at home mom or retiree.

In terms of broad economics and a return on value, intuition is ultimately sustainable. Paying attention to intuition and investing in intuition awareness in business requires low investment costs to generate potential high value outcomes. Companies and research facilities that invest in developing intuition tools and technologies ultimately stand to gain quantifiable innovation benefits, which may also lead to further intuition-mediated developments.

Intuition and Health

Clearly a more intuitive person has a greater likelihood of being in and maintaining a high level of personal health, lifestyle and well-being. Because of their intuitive alertness, they are more likely to be proactive, invest in self-care and make any necessary dietary or lifestyle changes. They are also less likely to maintain negative stress levels.

Health care costs can be minimized when intuitive approaches are able to stand alongside and sometimes displace traditional approaches where they are more effective. In the diagnostic field, intuitive healers and diagnosticians often work in tandem with medical practitioners and, where they do, are often able to spot things that routine medical analysis might miss. Of course, resistance and fear still exist in the medical profession and in society at large. When these views change as a result of greater understanding, everyone will benefit.

The potential contribution of intuition as both a diagnostic aid and an instrument of healing is large. The benefits of using intuition can be publicized and recognized by institutional leaders and professions. The application of intuitive diagnosis and healing needs to be balanced with respect for the belief systems and preferences of healing recipients along with respect for the extensive

system of peer-review and development that exists in medical science. In the scientific end of health research, the use of intuition will likely reveal substantive connections that foster radical innovations and better and more preventive approaches to health.

The development of peer-review systems for intuitive healers and practitioners would likely increase public acceptance and improve their recognition as professionals. Extensive communications and dialogue with medical professionals, licensing bodies, governments, health and insurance organizations are needed to help drive the understanding and acceptance of the unstructured

Instinctively we recognize the enormous power of having a connected world that can now distribute learning and awareness instantaneously, thereby having created the capability to immediately raise consciousness and know-how on any matter simultaneously. We have become one mind.

nature of intuitive work while ensuring that practitioners reflect a desired level of quality and experience.

Continued publication of success stories and examples of how alternative approaches are most effectively used will continue to make acceptance grow among the general population. Fusion approaches that encompass both Western and Eastern medical sciences will likely grow in popularity as their effective results become known.

Greater intuition is also needed in public health control so we can receive early and timely alerts in identifying potential instances of mass health risk or pandemics, and maximizing the communication and distribution of precautions and preventive practices.

Intuition, Ecology and Environment

It is through listening to the innate wisdom of our deeper intuition that we become more aware of our care-taking role over the living planet and its resources. Our collective intuition and the will to listen to it can identify the most effective approaches for managing and sharing resources, and restoring them for the benefit of all of us who share this planet.

Intuition, Public Security, and Conflict

Conflict and mediating our differences would still seem to be one of the largest impediments we face. Whether it is reconciling our differences one-on-one or drawing a line in the sand where two opposing units of a country or culture are engaged in the combat of difference, intuition has a role.

Here it becomes a clarifying agent, to distill the truth of remote separateness in the ways we see ourselves and the ways of seeing that we don't accept and to help create pathways, if not for acceptance, then at least for mutual remedies.

The more intuitive we become as individuals and as a global society, the better and harder we will work to find solutions in chaos, clarity in conflict and hope in reason. Through intuition, we will raise the questions we should be asking, and evolve together while appreciating the value of our differences. Perhaps, sooner than we think, we will celebrate them.

Resolving conflict is strong yet delicate work, where precedent doesn't always suggest a direction for the future. A well-developed intuitive sense would seem to be prerequisite for success for anyone working in this area. The best mediators, as it is generally known in the industry, do have a strong intuitive "nose" for their work. Academic approaches to mediation apply best in analyzing, reporting and documenting issues while actual field performance often performed without the luxury of extensive reflective time and analysis, is

Intuition is ultimately sustainable.

still the best predictor of future success. A well-developed intuition sense and timing often fill in the gaps.

As the demand for accountability and public administration continue to grow, two important areas of public administration stand out as fertile ground for the presence of intuitive reason: 1) Public security, in the perception and evaluation of potential security threats and 2) Health and Environmental Administration, in the assessment of potential health and pubic risks in the case of changing biological conditions, potential pandemics and threatening environments, such as weather warnings or contamination risks to air and water.

The use of intuition consultants to assist diagnostics in forensics and crimi-nal investigation has proven itself to be often useful, worthwhile and fruit-ful. A context-relevant, well-developed intuition sense for leaders and decision-makers could be extremely helpful for the effective handling of these cases, as could be the development of relevant Intuition-based Anticipation Models. Alternatively, they could solicit the use of intuitive consul-tants as a resource or to 'gut-proof' their strategies.

Intuition and Multi-Cultural Experience

All cultures are social experiments in humanity, centered around differing regions, shared histories, stories, cus-toms, language, beliefs, curiosities and preferences. While it is tempting to sug-gest that some cultures are more intui-tive than others, it is more interesting to find out how certain cultures are more intuitive, understand why this capacity developed, how their lives and lifestyles are affected and what we can learn from them.

Final Thoughts

The re-evaluation of intuition, increased development of intuition awareness in the general population, and greater research on the role of intuition in many areas of society, have merit and are likely to play a very significant and important role in shaping a more enlight-ened world. With innumerable appli-cations, tractable linkages, and innova-tive potential outcomes, establishing a new value for intuition will have a great impact on the world we choose to create tomorrow.

References

Revonsuo, A. (2009). *Inner presence: Consciousness as a biological phenomenon.* Cambridge, MA: The M.I.T. Press.

Sen, T. (2005). *Ancient secrets of success for today's world.* Toronto: Omnilux Publications.

Swami, D. (2009, April). Spiritual accounting (Lecture). University of Toronto.

Tesolin, A.L. (2009, February). Intuition as a sustainable business advantage. *Management Magazine.* Publication of the Certified Management Accountants, Canada, 15-16.

Painting in the Sky   Alex N. Moyer

I saw a painting on a wall inside a room
Violet 'I's gazed back at me through life's prism
Each stroke a modest touch of love's only song
Every color a star in the universe of being
Tears cried out to infinity behind art deco illustrations
Experience danced upon crystal canvas to the rhythm of meaning and absurdity
Divinity rained down upon the gardens of Self and soul over empty flowers
Synchronicity speaks to me as a soul mate, the painting a promise to Ourselves
awakened beyond simple stories of time and space

I am at a coffee shop
Paint runs over tables and people talking, dripping onto the ceiling
Disproportionate shapes and forms in unacceptable positions make love with
ordinary furniture in 3D space over invisible edges that span the universe

Moments become my paint as imagination swirls with the fire of Will
My heart becomes canvas where trees take root
I move the brush with my mind
As words, images, and emotions cover canvas with
the grace of sunlight upon an endless field

I made a painting on a wall inside a room
We made a painting on a wall inside a room

Alex N. Moyer is a computer graphic artist, writer, visionary, and integral creator. He works as a graphic and web designer with a focus on spiritual oriented projects. He is also interested in developing new ways for bringing greater awareness to our co-creational experiences on Earth.

Book Review

Rothberg, Donald. (2006). *The Engaged Spiritual Life: A Buddhist Approach to Transforming Ourselves and the World.*

Boston, Beacon Press. ISBN: 978-0807077252

Jonathan S. Watts

Some years ago, when I was working in the Secretariat of the International Network of Engaged Buddhists (INEB) in Bangkok, there was a young man who had come from Iceland and was looking for an idyllic Buddhist practice community. Like many of us Westerners, after reading so many Buddhist classics written over the last two and a half millennia, he thought such communities to be readily present all over Buddhist Asia. He was feeling a bit down one day when he came to our office, because he was finding that such a community was not so easy to find. So he asked me, "Jon, do you know a group that is really top notch? That is doing the best at integrating Buddhist values and practices with work for society? Because I want to go join that group. Can you tell me about that group?" I answered him with a bit of a laugh, insisting that, "If I knew such

a group, then I'd be working for them right now!"

This encounter points to one of the major issues addressed in Donald Rothberg's *The Engaged Spiritual Life*, an issue that many of us experience in both spiritual communities or more typical non-profits, (non-governmental organizations, or social action groups): how can the people who work in such high-minded organizations with lofty values, like saving the environment, stopping nuclear proliferation, or

> ## We need to be very careful not to project impossible idealisms onto high-minded organizations.

embodying the teachings of Jesus or Buddha in the world, be such egotistical, sexist, manipulating, narcissistic idiots?! Socially engaged Buddhism and other such spiritual social organizations have tried to answer this question, and their answer has been simply that many people in social change groups are quite imperfect precisely because (while working to effect outward social change) they avoid the equally important inner agenda of self-transformation. While the tenets of socially engaged Buddhism have always emphasized the

importance of engaging in inner development through meditation and other spiritual disciplines while engaging in outer social transformation, my own personal experience and the testaments of numerous people I know tell a different story: organizations created and run by our greatest socially engaged spiritual visionaries are rife with interpersonal problems.

This situation leads to two important realizations. The first is that we need to be very careful not to project impossible idealisms onto such organizations. Like our romantic tendency to imagine an ideal lover who exists somewhere out there but when we find him/her the ideal always seem to wane, many who have entered social activism, and particularly spiritually enthused social activism, have fallen under the spell of the myth of the enlightened guru and the enlightened ethos behind an organization. When we find out that the guru is also human and full of inconsistencies and contradictions and that the organization and its leaders are the same, we, just as we did with that old lover, write them off as fakers, charlatans and liars. The need to see through this illusion and to continually engage with the difficulties that confront us now leads to

Jonathan S. Watts has been working with the International Network of Engaged Buddhists (INEB) for the last twenty years. He coordinates Think Sangha, a socially engaged Buddhist think tank affiliated with INEB. He presently resides in Kamakura, Japan, where he is writing a book on socially engaged Buddhism in Japan and is also involved in spiritual preparation for death issues with the Jodo Shu Research Institute.

the second important point here. That is, we very much need what I would call "an intermediate practice" that can connect the psychological and spiritual, inner self-work that we do with the outer, social change work we do. This intermediate practice is what Rothberg calls the "relational domain." Between

Containers must be created for people to feel safe and willing to confront themselves.

the micro self of the individual and the macro collective self of society there is the intermediate self of the daily and often intimate relationships we engage in, from family to work place. These relationships are in many ways the real locus for our social engagement and for working out our personal agendas rather than the larger front of social action - such as the streets where we protest, the conferences that we attend, the classrooms where we teach. All of these latter places are where we put on our good face and receive accolades for our charm and prestigious backgrounds. However, it is within the trenches of our work places and homes that people see the real "us" in depth.

In every chapter of *The Engaged Spiritual Life*, Rothberg leads us into a social change issue that does not revolve around the crafting of ideology and the external issues which need to be confronted, but rather the critical means by which we engage in a holistic form of transformation that unites inner and out through the inter-relational. Rothberg sums up the essence of this idea by quoting Gandhi: "A non-violent revolution is not a program of seizure of power. It is a program of transformation of relationship" (p. 142). Likewise, each chapter in *The Engaged Spiritual Life* delves into a core relational competency, providing concrete practices for developing these competencies as 1) an inner practice, 2) a relational practice with others in daily contact and 3) a

social practice that hits at the structural and cultural systems of ignorance and injustice in the world.

The uniqueness of Rothberg's approach is seen in Chapter One, "Establishing the Conditions for Safety." This is a brilliant and essential starting point, because what so many personal and social change people don't understand is that the ego is far too resilient and tricky to change through force and coercion. The power of an ideology or of a well-oiled organizational machine will not create genuine social change; rather, attitudes and views—which in a Buddhist view are the very foundations of self and identity—must be confronted. Further, they must be confronted in a container where people feel empowered rather than threatened, able to be genuine and to speak from the higher self. The creation of such containers, as Rothberg understands and articulates, is the essential first step in the transformative process, a process which, according to the Buddha, must begin with an examination of one's suffering and one's connection to everyone's else's suffering. It is through this examination that the self can be disarmed of its ignorance, greed, and ill will. Containers must be created for people to feel safe and willing to confront themselves.

Chapter Three, "Clarifying and Setting Intentions," is another brilliant construction that shows the real depth of Rothberg's understanding of Buddhism. Although this book explicitly leans toward Buddhism, it is still imminently accessible because, like the Buddha himself, Rothberg discards the metaphysical assertions and trappings that Buddhism has taken on over the years and presents Buddhist teachings in a practical and ethical manner. For instance, the third chapter is essentially an explanation of Buddhist karma, yet there is not a moment where one starts to ponder whether one's being in this life is due to "my karma" from

some previous existence. Rather, Rothberg restates karma as the "clarifying of intentions" (karma in Buddhism literally means "intentional action") and then goes on to show how the creation, clarification and re-assertion of such intentions is the groundwork for moving forward in holistic transformation.

For myself, other highlights in the book that might especially be eye-opening for the non-Buddhist or non-spiritual activist include Chapter Five, "By Taking Care of Myself, I take Care of the World," which addresses the chronic problem of burnout and workaholism in social change organizations in which workers are in 24-7 crisis mode; Chapter Six, "Not Knowing but Keeping Going," which confronts the egoism of knowing it all and of controlling as much as possible, endemic in the internalized world view of fear in the modern age; and Chapter Eight, "Transforming Anger," which looks at how Buddhist meditation can enable one to experience pain and anger without

This is essential volume for anyone seeking to work through relational conflicts in their daily space and to unite their personal and social concerns.

reacting from that space.

In conclusion, *The Engaged Spiritual Life* is an extremely valuable "workbook," accessible for more secularly minded social activists to help ground their activism through developing a stronger inner life. It is also an essential volume for anyone seeking to work through relational conflicts in their daily space and to unite their personal and social concerns. This is a book that should not be read and then just catalogued on the bookshelf, but one that should eventually be worn away with marks, creases, post-its, the earmarks of an invaluable reference and resource as one engages in one's life and work.

www.ingramcontent.com/pod-product-compliance
Lightning Source LLC
Chambersburg PA
CBHW081724270326
41933CB00017B/3286